Library User Experience

SPEC KITS

Supporting Effective Library Management for Over Thirty-five Years

Committed to assisting research and academic libraries in the continuous improvement of management systems, ARL has worked since 1970 to gather and disseminate the best practices for library needs. As part of its commitment, ARL maintains an active publications program best known for its SPEC Kits. Through the Collaborative Research/Writing Program, librarians work with ARL staff to design SPEC surveys and write publications. Originally established as an information source for ARL member libraries, the SPEC Kit series has grown to serve the needs of the library community worldwide.

What are SPEC Kits?

Published six times per year, SPEC Kits contain the most valuable, up-to-date information on the latest issues of concern to libraries and librarians today. They are the result of a systematic survey of ARL member libraries on a particular topic related to current practice in the field. Each SPEC Kit contains an executive summary of the survey results; survey questions with tallies and selected comments; the best representative documents from survey participants, such as policies, procedures, handbooks, guidelines, Web sites, records, brochures, and statements; and a selected reading list—both print and online sources—containing the most current literature available on the topic for further study.

Subscribe to SPEC Kits

Subscribers tell us that the information contained in SPEC Kits is valuable to a variety of users, both inside and outside the library. SPEC Kit purchasers use the documentation found in SPEC Kits as a point of departure for research and problem solving because they lend immediate authority to proposals and set standards for designing programs or writing procedure statements. SPEC Kits also function as an important reference tool for library administrators, staff, students, and professionals in allied disciplines who may not have access to this kind of information.

SPEC Kits can be ordered directly from the ARL Publications Distribution Center. To order, call **(301) 362-8196**, fax **(301) 206-9789**, e-mail **pubs@arl.org**, or go to **http://www.arl.org/resources/pubs/**.

Information on SPEC Kits and the SPEC survey program can be found at **http://www.arl.org/resources/pubs/ spec/index.shtml**. The executive summary for each kit after December 1993 can be accessed free of charge at **http://www.arl.org/resources/pubs/spec/complete.shtml**.

SPEC Kit 322

Library User Experience

July 2011

Robert Fox

Dean of University Libraries

University of Louisville

Ameet Doshi

Assessment Coordinator and head of the User Experience Department

Georgia Tech

Association of Research Libraries

Series Editor: Lee Anne George

SPEC Kits are published by the

Association of Research Libraries
21 Dupont Circle, NW, Suite 800
Washington, DC 20036-1118
P (202) 296-2296 F (202) 872-0884
http://www.arl.org/resources/pubs/spec/
pubs@arl.org

ISSN 0160 3582

ISBN 1-59407-864-5
978-1-59407-864-4

Copyright © 2011

SPEC
Kit 322

Library User Experience

July 2011

SURVEY RESULTS

Executive Summary...11
Survey Questions and Responses...17
Responding Institutions 88

REPRESENTATIVE DOCUMENTS

User Experience Planning and Organization

Duke University
    Sharpening Our Vision.. 92
    Improving the User Experience 93
Georgia Tech
    Organization Chart 94
University of Michigan
    Information Technology. User Experience. Organization Chart.......................... 95

User Experience Projects

University of California, San Diego
    Assessment 98
Massachusetts Institute of Technology
    Libraries UX Group... 99
North Carolina State University
    User Studies at NCSU Libraries 101

Recruiting Volunteers

University of Colorado at Boulder
    Participants needed for library usability survey 104
    Study Title: Card Sort Activity on Library Research Help Guides 105
Columbia University
    Help improve the Libraries' website 107

University of Guelph

    New to the University of Guelph? 108

    Website Usability Study—Participants needed! 109

University of Virginia

    Website banner ad for Usability Testing 110

Web Usability

Duke University

    Web Assessment Reports 112

    Heatmaps of Key Library Pages: Spring 2011 113

Massachusetts Institute of Technology

    User Interface Group 115

    User Interface Group. Criteria for prioritizing our work 116

University of Michigan

    Usability in the Library 117

    Usability in the Library: Mirlyn (VuFind) Reports 119

Facility Design

Case Western Reserve University

    Student Competition: Redesign the First Floor of KSL.. 122

    Student Competition: Redesign the First Floor of KSL. Request for Proposals 124

    First Floor Architecture Drawing 129

University of Chicago

    Lighting and Laptop Survey 130

Georgia Tech

    Welcome to 2 West!... 132

    YouTube 2 West Charrette 134

Outreach

Georgia Tech

    "Lost in the Stacks" on WREK Radio 136

University of Notre Dame

    Senior Thesis Camp 138

Rice University

    The User Experience Office (UX) libguide 140

Vanderbilt University

    Library Renovation guide 141

User Feedback

University of Chicago

    Surveys 144

    2010 Survey of graduate and professional school students 145

University of Kansas
    Snapshot Day at Anschutz Library, April 14, 2010 146
Massachusetts Institute of Technology
    Ethnographic study – Digital Scholarship at MIT 148
Northwestern University
    Library Feedback 152
Rice University
    Establishing fondren@brc 153
Rutgers University
    Summary. New Brunswick Student Focus Groups, Spring 2008 158
    Ethnographic Research Project: Reports 160
    Studying Students to Enhance Library Services at Rutgers University 161
University of Washington
    UW Libraries Assessment 167
    In Library Use Surveys 168
    In Library Use Survey 2008. Branch Library 170
University of Waterloo
    Porter Main Floor Renovation. Furniture Charrette – Summary of Results 171
    Porter Main Floor Renovation. Informal Interview 174
    Porter Main Floor Renovation. Feedback request card 175

Advisory Boards
University of British Columbia
    Advisory Committee 178
University of Chicago
    Library Student Resource Group 180
Georgia Tech
    Faculty Advisory Board 181
University of North Carolina at Chapel Hill
    University Library Student Library Advisory Board 182
York University
    Library Student Advisory Group 184

Job Descriptions
Georgia Tech
    User Engagement Librarian/Assessment Coordinator 186
University of Guelph
    User Experience Librarian 187
Johns Hopkins University
    User Experience Director 190
University of Michigan
    User Experience (UX) Specialist 192

SELECTED RESOURCES

Books and Articles 197

Websites and Blogs 198

Twitter Sites 199

SURVEY RESULTS

EXECUTIVE SUMMARY

What is UX?

The term "User Experience" (UX) originally emerged from the web usability and application interface design community. Over the past few years, other service-oriented industries, such as the marketing and retail services community, have adopted the term as a holistic approach to describe designing the ideal customer experience. More recently, innovators have applied the design of such experiences to libraries. As Aaron Schmidt points out in his *Library Journal* column about the user experience, a goal for UX design is to minimize "pain" points throughout library processes, whether they are physical (library facilities, for example) or digital experiences (Schmidt, 2010). Furthermore, user experience as applied to the research library includes both the traditional customer service approach of reacting to user concerns, as well as proactively including users in the library design and strategic planning process by employing a variety of means, including focus groups and advisory boards.

A review of the literature suggests that there is a lack of controlled vocabulary when defining user experience within the library context. This is a relatively new field with little standardization, especially in academic or library environments. As a result, and as the data from this survey demonstrates, user experience is interpreted to include a wide range of activities in library organizations, including but not limited to assessment, user engagement, library design, outreach, and marketing. As Knemeyer writes in "Defining Experience," *everything* a company produces should be viewed through the lens of the user's experience (2008). Therefore, every part of the organization has a stake in improving that experience. Research libraries are beginning to adopt this integrative design approach and develop unique organizational structures to manage the user experience.

The Survey

The purpose of this survey was to explore recent and planned user experience activities at ARL member libraries and the impact these efforts have on helping the libraries transform to meet evolving user needs. The survey elicited examples of successful user experience activities to serve as benchmarks for libraries looking to create or expand efforts in this area. It also explored whether libraries have created positions or entire departments focused on user engagement and the user experience. The survey was conducted between February 7 and March 4, 2011. Seventy-one of the 126 ARL member libraries completed the survey for a response rate of 56%.

User Experience Projects/Feedback Opportunities

All but one of the survey respondents indicated that they engaged in at least one user experience project or activity over the past three years. Most of these past activities were both project-based and on-going. Almost all of the respondents report they plan to engage in at least one user experience activity in the coming year. As with the past UX activities, a large majority indicated that future activities would also be both ongoing and project-based. Below are some examples of future activities:

- Our metadata and collections units are developing a User Experience Team to develop usability assessment and evaluation tools as well as run focus groups with various campus groups (students and faculty) to better understand user needs and information seeking behaviors as discovery systems and collections continue to be amalgamated, redesigned, and/or acquired.

- Strategic planning, website usability, and OPAC usability testing.
- We plan an observational study of our library spaces in the spring of 2011, and an ethnographic study of how scholarly methods are changing due to new technologies and formats, also in Spring 2011.
- We will be starting a summer study of how researchers do their scholarly work, with a special emphasis on data management needs.

The survey asked respondents to select up to two user experience activities the library had recently undertaken that had the biggest impact or were most innovative. They were then asked a set of questions about those activities. They described 121 different activities. Many respondents reported on activities to solicit user input related to building renovation and redesign. Other UX projects included assessing the OPAC, user input regarding access to electronic resources, and general website usability.

Respondents were asked to describe techniques and tools they used to gather user input. The most frequently mentioned tool was surveys. The simplest were homegrown instruments that were printed and distributed in libraries or that were created using web survey sites. The most commonly mentioned survey tool was LibQUAL+® or a variant such as LibQUAL+® Lite. Many respondents indicated they regularly use LibQUAL+® every two to three years, creating a set of longitudinal data. A number of respondents also noted that they employ LibQUAL+® to identify broad areas of user concern and then utilize focus groups or targeted surveys to further understand those areas of concern.

Combined, the passive techniques of gathering anecdotal user comments or suggestions received physically or online were the second most frequently mentioned form of user input. Nearly two-thirds of the examples cited by respondents incorporated this type of feedback at some point in the data collection process.

Half of the UX activities used focus groups and a third employed some form of usability testing. The latter technique was used primarily for redesigning websites. As might be expected, more labor intensive techniques, such as individual interviews and observations, were not cited as frequently; their use was noted in ten and five per cent of the responses, respectively.

For approximately half of the examples, respondents used a combination of both open recruitment and direct invitations to solicit participants for feedback. A fourth used open recruitment only and the other fourth used direct invitation only. The survey data indicates that libraries used a variety of techniques to recruit participants. The most frequently mentioned example was e-mail, closely followed by an invitation on the library's web page or personal contact from a library employee. More than half of the respondents used all three of these approaches. Around a quarter of the respondents used social media tools, and a like number used in-house media, such as a library newsletter, in their recruitment. Libraries planning to recruit feedback participants should budget for some type of incentive, as over 70% of respondents indicated that they provided incentives. The most common incentives were food and gift cards. Nearly three-quarters of the respondents indicated that the costs associated with their feedback projects were borne by the library's operating budget; the remainder were financed by library foundation funds or special, one-time funding such as a grant.

Funds spent on soliciting user feedback seemed to generate a high return on investment; 43% of respondents noted that the feedback led to a complete redesign of, or major modifications to, library services or spaces. Another 39% noted that the feedback led to minor modifications to existing services or spaces.

For nearly 90% of the projects mentioned, libraries reported feedback results to important constituencies, such as users and library administration and staff. Also, many respondents indicated that they share survey results and other products of user experience activities in written form with institutional governing bodies. Examples include:

- Library of Congress Executive Committee and Management
- Data used in budget presentations to the President's Executive Team
- Campus Renovation Committee
- Senior levels of the university administration via the library's annual report
- The Learning Commons design process mentioned in the annual report and in the faculty newsletter
- Institutional Research Planning

Some respondents also indicated they share results within the library community via conference presentation and publication. For example:

- Conference presentations (IUG, ALA Annual, and possibly IFLA) as well as an intended article for *Library Trends*
- Publishing the results more broadly, e.g., in an academic article
- Communicating to the broader academic library community through conference presentations

A smaller number indicated they share results with the general user community via more widespread and public means such as social media, posting results on websites, and through the use of open forums.

Organizational Structure

Several questions in the survey sought information on how libraries organized activities and staffed positions related to assessment and, more specifically, the user experience. Nearly all respondents indicated that their library at least periodically conducts assessment activities, but a surprising number indicated no formal assessment structure in their organization. Most respondents indicated that assessment activities were often ad hoc and conducted by one or more library units that hoped to benefit from the particular information sought. Still, half of the respondents reported a dedicated Assessment Coordinator position, and a quarter identified a dedicated position focusing on user experience. Based on respondent comments, one

might expect a future upward trend for these types of positions. Numerous comments alluded to new or recently revitalized assessment efforts and new organizational structures and personnel to support such programs. The comments also indicated a very broad and growing awareness of the need to have activities focused solely on measuring and improving user experience. Indeed, while many respondents noted that user experience efforts were but one component of a broader assessment program, the importance of the user experience component appears to be growing substantially. One particularly appropriate comment demonstrating this trend is the following:

> (UX activities) are the heart of our assessment activities. Most of our other "assessment" activities are merely keeping statistics about usage and involve very little actual assessment at this point in time.

As noted above, many of the responding libraries do not currently have one person dedicated to coordinating an assessment or user experience program. An inherent danger in not having a coordinator is the potential lack of a consistent message or brand in this area. In general though, responding libraries seem to have some awareness of this issue and have assigned fairly high-level supervision here. When asked to name who in their library has primary oversight of user experience activities, libraries that do not have dedicated user experience and/or assessment coordinators routinely indicated oversight by another department head level position or by someone at the associate dean/AUL level. When asked to whom this coordinator reports, over three quarters of the respondents indicated the coordinator reported to someone at the dean or associate dean level.

Strategic Planning

While there was not a specific question about it in the survey, a number of respondents referred to the library strategic plan or planning process. Several comments noted how user experience, or in a broader context, assessment activities provided input into their most recent strategic plan. Two respondents specifically mentioned the use of focus groups for user input, while one noted individual faculty interviews. Two respondents also remarked that their student advisory boards provided input during this process, and one indicated that their University Library Committee reviewed strategic directions. On the output side, a number of respondents indicated that user experience and/or assessment were identified as strategic priorities or as action items within their recent strategic plans. One respondent noted that library user experience activities were funded by their parent institution as a part of the campus strategic plan. While the total number of references to strategic plans was limited, we might expect to see an increased emphasis on user experience and assessment activities in strategic plans as the UX field matures and becomes more commonplace in research library agendas.

Advisory Boards

Over 80% of the respondents indicated that they had some type of formal advisory board in place. In their responses they described 117 separate boards, of which 60 were composed solely of students. Half of the student boards included both undergraduate and graduate members, or the respondent noted only that the board had student members but made no distinction on their classification. The other half of the student boards was split almost evenly between "undergraduates only" and "graduates only." Nearly all the student boards were noted as providing a mechanism for student advice and input. When asked what specific outcomes resulted from these boards, respondents noted three primary areas: general input on policies and services, review of and possible extension of service hours, and input on library renovation and space utilization, especially as it pertained to the creation of quiet study zones.

Thirty-three of the advisory boards were composed of faculty only or a combination of faculty and staff. The majority of these boards were considered to be of an advisory nature, although a few had targeted missions. When asked about outcomes here, respondents indicated that for nearly half the boards the primary outcome was establishing and maintaining communication between the faculty and library administration. Interestingly, a fourth of the faculty boards had no outcomes listed at all. The

remaining boards had outcomes listed of improving services and collections, reviewing and/or approving proposed policy changes, and assistance in survey development.

Sixteen boards were composed of faculty and student members. The most common faculty/student board structure reported was of a faculty senate committee that included limited student representation. Notably, these boards more closely resembled faculty-only boards than student-only boards in their roles and outcomes. Two-thirds of the respondents indicated the primary board role was advisory in nature, and two-thirds associated no specific outcomes as a result of the board.

Eight of the boards did not include student members and had little or no faculty representation. These boards were primarily associated with library development efforts.

Based on the information submitted in this survey, it appears that a majority of boards associated with user engagement activities contain only student members. For the most part, respondents noted well-defined roles and outcomes for these boards. Boards composed only of faculty members or faculty members with limited student participation were often viewed as important communication tools but had less well-defined outcomes or no outcomes noted at all. Institutions seeking active student input on user experience activities may be better served by the use of student-only boards rather than boards with limited student participation.

Summary

This survey revealed that nearly all responding ARL member institutions are employing a form of user engagement, whether or not they refer to it as such. For some libraries, the activities may be limited to small surveys or perhaps a focus group, while other libraries are engaging users through formal advisory boards and are sponsoring comprehensive ethnographic studies. Organizationally, the responding libraries range from an institution with no formal assessment program that periodically conducts ad hoc exercises to an institution with a user experience department. While there appears to be a lack of common vocabulary or program standardization, there is a growing awareness of the need to assess libraries from the user perspective with new positions and even departments created to accomplish this goal.

It is clear that creating the structure to measure and change the user experience takes time and effort. As one respondent noted, "You can't just suddenly tell staff 'Ok, today we have a new user experience' and expect everyone to jump on the bandwagon. I hope in your study you will communicate that making this transition to a UX culture takes time and staff have to be ready to move forward because they believe in it, not because an administrator says we need a new UX or because we created a UX librarian position."

Overall, respondents feel that efforts made in assessing the user experience are well spent. They articulated numerous projects that resulted in major program updates and facility revisions and that were well received by library administration, governing/funding boards, and most importantly, by library users.

These trends are significant because it suggests that user experience activities have been adopted by almost all respondents, and furthermore, that these activities and projects are long term in nature. Thus, the trends point to a present and future with UX activities more central to the operations of ARL libraries.

SURVEY QUESTIONS AND RESPONSES

The SPEC survey on the Library User Experience was designed by **Robert Fox**, Dean of University Libraries, University of Louisville, and **Ameet Doshi**, Assessment Coordinator and head of the User Experience Department, Georgia Tech. These results are based on data submitted by 71 of the 126 ARL member libraries (56%) by the deadline of March 4, 2011. The survey's introductory text and questions are reproduced below, followed by the response data and selected comments from the respondents.

Research libraries find themselves increasingly being asked to justify program expenditures in terms of their impact on research, teaching, and learning activities. An important aspect in generating high impact for the library is ensuring that its resources and services closely align with the evolving needs of its users. Libraries may engage their users through a number of methods to help create this alignment, including formal and informal evaluation tools, outreach efforts to specific user groups, and feedback from user advisory boards. Research libraries have a long history of evaluating collection needs and general user satisfaction. More recently, assessment has adopted a user-centered mindset focused on evaluation of the user experience for improving the design of library services and facilities. As Aaron Schmidt describes in the *Library Journal* User Experience column:

> "Touch points are all the places your patrons come into contact with your library and its services. Things like your web site and databases, service desks, staff, programs, and even brochures. One goal of User Experience Design is to help determine if any of those touch points are also pain points—places of contact that make patrons confused, aggravated, or disappointed—and fix them if they are." (May 1, 2010)

The purpose of this survey is to explore recent and planned user experience activities at ARL member libraries and the impact these efforts have on helping the libraries transform to meet evolving user needs. The survey elicits examples of successful user experience activities to serve as benchmarks for libraries looking to create or expand efforts in this area. It also explores whether libraries have created positions or entire departments focused on user engagement and the user experience.

Definitions
In this survey, "users" include anyone who utilizes or could reasonably be expected to utilize the library's services and resources, for example, students, faculty, researchers, and community members. "User experience activities" includes any effort by the library to:

1. Assess or measure the experience users encounter with the library's services, resources, facilities, and technology;
2. Seek user input to help design or guide improvements in these same areas;
3. Collaborate with other library staff or campus/community partners to enhance library services, facilities, and resources in innovative ways;
4. Utilize advisory boards and/or outreach efforts to gain a better understanding of user needs.

1. Has your library engaged in any user experience activities as defined in the introduction during the past three years? (Examples include administering surveys, facilitating advisory boards, leading outreach activities, creating user experience positions/units, etc.) N=71

Yes	70	99%
No	1	1%

If yes, were these activities one-time/project-based or ongoing or both? N=69

Project-based	7	10%
Ongoing	6	9%
Both	56	81%

Comments

Project-based

Evaluation of the Visitor Experience at the Library of Congress.

Planning for development of new Taylor Family Digital Library that brings together library, archives, museum, and press together in new ways and also brings Student Services into the building and more solidly in the mix of services. Planning a renovation of our Health Sciences Library. Both projects involved research on the user experience.

We've used surveys of users in both paper and electronic formats, including LibQUAL+® and in-house surveys.

Ongoing

Our efforts are pretty much focused on outreach activities.

Student assessment of library skills course; active marketing department.

Both

A UX Librarian position was created in October 2009. We administered the LibQUAL+® Lite survey in the spring of 2010. In addition, a UX office, a physical space, was created in January 2010. The UX office has collaborated across departments to do informal surveys, as well as, an ethnographic study of the research activities in one building on campus.

At the J. Willard Marriott Library, we do a biennial Library Satisfaction survey in the spring semester about activity and satisfaction within the library. The Library Satisfaction survey is a one page print survey completed inside the Marriott Library gathering demographic information such as major, department, and visitor type. Most questions on this survey use a Likert scale with a couple of open-ended questions for comments. The LibQUAL+® survey is done every four years. We have done focus groups to gather more data on specific issues from LibQUAL+® data. The library has done surveys in the past regarding a specific project or idea. Surveys, consultants, focus groups, student groups, university committees, planning task forces, furniture trials, outside committees were extensively used from 2004 until 2007 in the planning and renovation of an 80 million project at the J. Willard Marriott Library. Since 2007, survey topics include website redesign, library catalog redesign, hours within the library, and services and food quality in the café. The library has done transaction log analysis on catalog searches, interlibrary loan, website, collections, databases, and journals. In 2010, the library created a usability lab that has been used to test our library catalog and website. With the library website being moved to a new platform, online surveys will be much easier to create, implement, gather, and analyze data. The library has a Library Policy Advisory Committee that provides suggestions on new initiatives.

Broad categories include administration of surveys, advisory boards, usability testing, and various outreach activities.

LibQUAL+® in 2003, 2006, 2009; Student Advisory Group, Outreach Group, created a campus outreach coordinator to work primarily with freshmen, Assessment Group.

Project based have included the LibQUAL+® survey, website usability testing which led to a website redesign, and a strategic planning process. Ongoing includes liaison work to academic departments and the Library Affairs Advisory Committee, which has been around for many years and consists of faculty and sometimes student reps.

South (main) Reading Room study; Special Collections use study; Portland Library & Learning Commons user focus groups; usability testing for portions of the website (faculty services page, digital collections; WorldCat local); furniture evaluations; focus groups on new media studies; data services needs assessment; LibQUAL+®; Student Advisory Group; University Library Committee; Library Advancement Council.

The library has participated in two LibQUAL+® surveys—one in 2007 and one in 2010. This is an ongoing process, with surveys held every three years. The library has been holding interviews with college deans and associate deans as well as student groups to determine ways to improve the user experience. The library is also piloting a peer-assisted learning program.

The Penn Libraries facilitate a number of ongoing advisory groups, including groups of undergraduate students, life sciences faculty, and faculty in the humanities. We also conduct project-based focus groups and usability studies with university faculty, staff, and student advisory bodies to gauge their perceptions of and facility with library services and technologies.

Usability is ongoing and we are currently mid-way through a refresher of our Undergraduate Research Project. We also did a user study on the Carlson Science and Engineering Library.

Vast majority are project-based.

We conduct the LibQUAL+® survey every two years as well as targeted surveys, usability studies, and focus groups.

We conducted an annual user services survey, usually in the spring term. Additionally, we participated in the Kansas State Library Annual "Snapshot" day survey (April 2010 and November 2010). We also recently launched a new Learning Studio facility, and have conducted focus groups, surveys, comment and voting opportunities, and ethnographic observational studies related to this project. Additionally, Digital Initiatives and Publishing has historically employed user advisory boards for services like the institutional repository, a journal editor's board to talk about issues with open access, an advisory board for shared digital image collections. Recently, we partnered with the campus humanities research center to co-lead a year-long advisory group to better understand the needs of humanists working in the digital realm. This work included both focused discussion and survey. Most recently, we utilized campus focus groups to help faculty understand the implications of KU's new open access policy, and have subsequently established an ongoing advisory board for that group. In the area of library collections, we have met with multiple academic departments to gather input as we physically move collections to the annex.

We do usability testing every year and a large user survey every two years. We also conduct ethnographic studies, but the last one was in 2006, so won't be discussed in this survey. The next one will be in spring 2011.

We don't call it "User Experience" at BYU, but we do the activities defined in the questions above.

We have done several of each, surveys and boards. We have faculty and student boards. We have done focus groups with students. I personally make visits to department chairs to ask them about their experience with the library – it's an open-ended conversation that is sometimes attended by faculty. More important, at our public services retreat in July 2010 our topic was customer service and user experience. This was the launch of a conversation in public services about the differences between customer service and user experience. This is an ongoing project. For example, on January 14, 2011 we had a 90 minute program where we watched video by user experience consultant Joe Michelli, had lightning talks by staff on service issues, and started something we call "Capture an Idea" project. Back in the fall of 2010, our head of reference attended an ethnographic research workshop, and we are now planning our first study which will focus on faculty and how they create links to library content on their course sites.

We have done surveys, focus groups, a faculty advisory committee, outreach to campus organizations.

We utilize a year round online survey as well as an annual print survey.

2. Does your library have plans to engage in any user experience activities in the coming year? N=71

Yes	69	97%
No	2	3%

If yes, will these activities be one-time/project-based or ongoing or both? N=69

Project-based	7	10%
Ongoing	5	7%
Both	57	83%

Comments

Project-based

We're in the planning phases for more focus groups and surveys.

Ongoing

My hope is to increase our assessment activities and add an assessment coordinator to keep those activities focused and effective.

We will have a "Capture an Idea" project in which staff have special notebooks to record things that are broken, observations of users, comments, complaints; we have student workers participating as well. Before we can understand what the library user experience should be, we need to understand what it is now and how we go about designing it to be better. This is part of an ongoing effort to create more staff awareness about UX in the library. You can't just suddenly tell staff "Ok, today we have a new user experience" and expect everyone to jump on the bandwagon. I hope in your study you will communicate that making this transition to a UX culture takes time and staff have to be ready to move forward because they believe in it, not because an administrator says we need a new UX or because we created a UX librarian position. My goal has been to start slow and more carefully, seeking to build staff support along the way. Part of that is retreats, meetings, videos, sharing news, interactive projects in which everyone can participate, etc., all designed to create awareness and an interest in the importance of having a well designed library experience.

Both

Cafe Gelman, Ear Plugs for Reading Days, student orientation sessions, Student Advisory Group to work with library and university staff on planning Gelman Library's 1st floor renovation.

Comprehensive usability testing of the website is likely. Advisory groups will continue to meet. Other activities are not yet specified, but likely.

Continuation of activities outlined above with the addition of focus groups around the implementation of strategic planning initiatives.

Currently reviewing how students wish to access reference service. Looking at putting in place a resource discovery layer to assist users in accessing information resources. Installing a "suggestion box." Establish a customer service committee.

Our assessment program has been in a rebuilding phase. Hope to return to ongoing program of activities in the future, but most will still be project-based.

Our metadata and collections units are developing a User Experience Team to develop usability assessment and evaluation tools as well as run focus groups with various campus groups (students and faculty) to better understand user needs and information seeking behaviours as discovery systems and collections continue to be amalgamated, redesigned, and/or acquired.

Strategic planning, website usability, and OPAC usability testing.

Usability and Undergraduate Research Refresher projects.

We are implementing a new strategic plan over the next 3 to 6 months, which will include metrics.

We plan an observational study of our library spaces in the spring of 2011, and an ethnographic study of how scholarly methods are changing due to new technologies and formats, also in spring 2011.

We plan to complete our biennial in-building survey, and others as may arise.

We will be conducting LibQUAL+® in 2012 as well as focused surveys in the college and departmental libraries and our annual Info Commons survey.

We will be starting a summer study of how researchers do their scholarly work, with a special emphasis on data management needs.

We will be validating a redesign of our periodicals room with students. We are also doing LibQUAL+®.

If you answered "Yes" to either question above, please complete the survey. If you answered "No" to both questions, please jump to the Other Outreach Activities section.

3. How do your library user experience activities fit within the library's broader array of assessment activities? N=59

According to our library's mission statement, the library must "understand the research, teaching, and learning needs of its users" in order to fulfill its mission. The desire to understand the experience and needs of library users is perhaps the raison d'être for the library's assessment program. There is substantial overlap between the library's user experience activities and its assessment activities, though they are not wholly coterminous.

All of our assessment activities are currently focused on our users.

Assessment of customer needs and assessment of the customer are the central components of our assessment activities. We assess needs to determine what our customers need from us to support their success. This information informs our strategic planning and development of new services or resources. Assessment of the user experience (including satisfaction with our services) helps us assess our progress toward our goals and helps identify areas in need of improvement. Our other assessment activities are primarily clustered around efficiency in use of our resources and staff climate and learning needs.

At this time, the library does not have a designated assessment unit, or a user experience unit, so these activities are generally done at the department or division level, in alignment with strategic priorities.

Currently, the majority of our assessment activities are focused on user experience with services that currently exist or on identifying gaps in services that would enhance user experience. However, we do "by the number" assessment of ILL/resource sharing, cataloging, and other production areas of the libraries to meet goals.

For many years, we have had a committee that administers surveys and works on branding and marketing issues. The UX office works with the chair of that committee to coordinate and report on survey activities. The UX office coordinates the library's marketing efforts, promotes outreach, and leads the web team's usability testing. Additionally, the UX office engages with users via focus groups, and informal surveys.

GWUL responded to LibQUAL+® results by creating position of Student Liaison who works with the AUL for Administration, Development, and Human Resources, and with the Outreach Group to plan and participate in several annual student centered activities. Examples are new student orientations during summer before freshman year, graduate student orientations, resident advisors assistance, "Take a Break" activities with snacks, fun giveaways, movies, etc.

I tend to view "user experience" activities as an attempt to capture feedback on a more narrowly defined basis, e.g., on a particular service or space, from a particular user group.

In 2002 and 2006, the UIC University Library participated in the LibQUAL+® Total Service Quality survey. The surveys highlighted a need for greater access to technology and overall improvements to library facilities (which had not been renovated since the 1980s). As a result, over the last several years, the library has conducted multiple user surveys focusing on experience with reference, instruction, circulation, and collections. Additionally, an annual user survey is conducted during the fall semester to measure library performance and patron satisfaction, with a particular emphasis on facilities, services, and technological resources. It has tracked satisfaction and improvement in these areas, while also gathering useful information about changing patron wants and needs. In response to patron feedback, the library has made significant changes. Over the past 18 months, library hours have been extended, physical improvements have been made in all facilities, and public computers have been replaced and upgraded. Later this year, construction will begin on a new IDEA Commons—a space intended for active learning and 24 hour access. Information gained is also being used to make strategic decisions about collections development and allocation of resources. The annual survey also provides respondents the opportunity to identify what they feel should be priorities for the library. Responses have centered on continuing to improve the physical space and increasing access to technology and online services and resources. Together, this information helps the library focus its resources to responsively meet the varied needs of its users, while also ensuring that it is fulfilling its mission to support, enhance, and collaborate in the education, research, and service activities of the university. The UIC University Library is committed to ongoing assessment in order to best serve its users. Future assessment activities will continue to focus on the user experience, including plans for: a new comprehensive user survey evaluating satisfaction with services and resources; improved instruction evaluation tools; new in-depth reference assessment tools; and the introduction of online and physical suggestion boxes. Additionally, all current and future assessment activities will be complemented by a new marketing campaign aiming to better communicate assessment efforts and subsequent improvements with users, while also building a greater culture of assessment library-wide.

In addition to user experience activities, NARA also complies with the Government Performance and Results Act of 1993 (GPRA). In doing so, we survey virtually all users of NARA staff-provided services, and report these results to Congress.

Integrated—all part of administrative efforts at assessment.

It is one aspect of many, but in a "where the rubber hits the road" sort of way.

It's really the centerpiece in many ways; almost everything you want to measure or improve has to do with the users.

Members of the library's Assessment Team consult on user experience activities and conduct assessments of their own. The Team has worked to establish a culture of assessment so more individuals have taken responsibility for assessing their activities.

Most of our assessment activities fall into the category of "user experience" even though we might not call it that. Like most libraries, we do focus groups, surveys, usability testing, etc., but there is no formal assessment program or plan to guide these assessment activities.

Most of the activities of my department are involved in one way or the other with the user experience—either virtual or physical use of the library. There are other data kept by separate departments that are reported annually, but we don't act on these very much. These are things like data reported to ARL.

Much of the assessment is identified and conducted by library departments that have specific assessment needs, with support (as needed) from the User Feedback & Assessment Committee.

Our assessment program relies on multiple methods to provide information about our community's library and information needs, use, importance, and satisfaction on both an ongoing and project basis. We find that qualitative methods focusing on the user experience are absolutely critical in gaining student input.

Our intent is to develop assessment efforts this next year, as part of our strategic planning efforts. Assessment will primarily focus on user experiences.

Our library has a department dedicated to analyzing and improving the User Experience. Assessment is a major component of the User Experience department's role, but other activities also include: facilitating an active student library advisory board, conducting outreach with users outside the library, collaborating with innovative campus partners, facilitating focus groups, monitoring and engaging with users on social media feeds, and performing both systematic and ad hoc surveys with students in library spaces.

Our most recent strategic plan includes the goal of improving the user experience.

Our user experience activities are "Actions" tied to the goals and objectives of our strategic plan. The measure of the success of the "Action" is an assessment activity.

Our user experience activities are an integral part of the library's broader array of assessment activities. Assessment is seen as a strategic priority both for the institution and the library. Data-driven decision making is essential in a resource-limited environment.

Piloting assessment for a user-centered library.

Some user experience activities are coordinated through the Libraries' Director of Planning, Assessment, and Research. Others are initiated as part of the regular management and improvement of Public Services.

"Student learning" and "community engagement" are two of the main strategic directions of the UBC Library Strategic Plan 2010–2015. The Assessment Program is designated as one of two "critical enablers" (the other is IT). The Assessment Office and Assessment Advisory Group identify activities and services to support the assessment goals of the Assessment Office, library-wide assessment projects, and unit plans at the branch/division level. In addition to the third LibQUAL+® survey of 2010, the library user experience has been the focus of at least a dozen smaller assessment projects in the last year (either completed, or in progress), including projects to redesign user spaces, improve the library website, and provide better access to collections. Results of the LibQUAL+® 2010 survey have been shared with public service managers, management committees, and with library staff in open forums.

The BC Libraries are in the midst of significant change related to the User Experience. Many of our current initiatives stem from our deep and wide discussions of our organizational culture. These discussions allowed us to really examine how we deploy all the resources (Web, desk, services, etc.) where users interface with us. The library continues to look at ways to improve the user experience—including building renovations and space allocation, student assessments of library instruction.

The library's user experience activities help to highlight the efficiency of the varied services offered to students as well as to identify those services that are not as effective in meeting users' needs. "Ineffective" areas are reported and acted upon by the senior staff so that they can be redressed to meet user needs. Within the broader array of assessment activities, user experience problems are taken seriously and are focused on to find a solution.

The Penn State Libraries assesses users' evaluative feedback on online and physical services, including the libraries' website, special outreach programs, and reference and instruction initiatives. These assessments complement the libraries' broader array of assessment activities by showing the impact of the libraries' collections, resources, staff, and services on library use and user satisfaction.

There is at most only a loose coupling in that I am responsible for both assessment and building our UX culture (and assessment culture). I think at this point we are looking at designing and implementing the UX concept outside of our more traditional assessment activity. I would hope that we can get to the point where we could begin to assess the impact of our UX, but before we can evaluate the library experience we have to define it, design it, and integrate it into our practice. Even UX experts struggle with assessment matters, because it is difficult to assess how much impact the experience has on community members. But we can perhaps assess this in other ways, perhaps more traditional satisfaction surveys, focus groups, and ethnographic methods.

There is strong collaboration between Management Information Services (MIS), UVa Library's general assessment office, and the User Experience Team, which does more targeted user studies. A faculty member of MIS serves on the UX Team and serves as convener of the User Requirements/Usability Community.

They are a regular part of the assessment activities.

They are an integral part of our assessment activities. Our assessment librarian spends 20% of her time in the User Experience Group and helps coordinate user experience activities with other assessment activities.

They are an important component, since responding to users' needs is a core value of the organization.

They are an integral piece of our assessment program.

They are currently the major priority, as they are driving changes to the library's website and v-reference hours, for example. We do sporadic "who is using this library" surveys, but they don't necessarily drive change.

They are one aspect of our assessment activities which include usability studies, process reviews, unit reviews, customer satisfaction surveys, focus groups, Information Literacy assessments, Reference Studies, and ACRL, ALA, NCES, and ARL projects.

They are the heart of our assessment activities. Most of our other "assessment" activities are merely keeping statistics about usage and involve very little actual assessment at this point in time.

They are vehicles for feedback on certain issues. We are employing them in planning library services (e.g., 24 hour library service) and space (Learning Commons).

This is all fairly new to our library. We understand the importance, but still need to integrate it into the organization.

To be honest, I think we are currently woefully inadequate across our whole system in finding out whether we are doing well or not.

User experience activities are a part of the assessment activities coordinated by our Planning and Assessment Officer. The user experience and the quality of the experience is part of our new strategic planning document for 2011–2014. User experience will be taking a more prominent role since our library finally completed a massive innovation/renovation project costing 80 million dollars. User experiences that we hope to measure include all aspects of library operations ranging from group study areas, computer usage, website, resource allocation, user environment, ease of navigation within the library and the library website, resource availability, hours, and collection development priorities.

User experience activities are integral to assessment and strategic management of the Penn Libraries' resources, services, and technologies. While we have a central office that oversees planning and assessment activities, library user experience activities are distributed throughout library staff and locations.

User experience activities are planned as appropriate to the question asked.

User experience activities complement and/or extend results of studies conducted as part of broader program, e.g., LibQUAL+®, WOREP, READ, Project Information Literacy.

User experience activities complement other forms of assessment. They may or may not be part of the portfolio of the Assessment Team.

User experience assessments are intended to help us understand user frustrations, expectations, challenges, needs and more. Such assessments may inform the development modification or elimination of services, or may be conducted in order to make necessary changes with the least amount of negative impact on the user.

User experience is one prong of our assessment program, but is the largest focus.

We are hoping to build an overall assessment plan as well as a culture of assessment. The activities in which we will engage in the near future will focus on creating and improving web-based services.

We are in the early stages of assessment planning on a broad and systematic scale.

We do more of this kind of assessment than any other.

We do not have a formal assessment program at UM but we do have a wide range of assessment activities. The most formal and ongoing work is done via the User Experience Department (a department within the Library Information Technology unit). There are also occasional assessment activities in the Technical Services unit and in Public Services.

The UX Department primarily focuses on UX for the online library presence but also advises in many of the public services department projects.

We do not have a formal assessment program so user experience is done with ad hoc teams by staff who have an interest in, and experience with, assessment.

We employ some activities to acquire data for decision-making purposes, but we also employ some activities as more general listening devices.

We have a three-member user experience team whose role and scope is still being defined. We also have an Assessment & Evaluation team, and one member of the UX team sits on it. At present, it seems the UX team is involved in qualitative research and A&E is more concerned with quantitative research.

We have system stats to help determine the use of existing systems, but we rely on user experience to assess planned and recent system changes, and to help with creation of future services and spaces.

Western Libraries participates in large scale projects such as LibQUAL+® to identify where users have concerns, and then works towards improving service/resources as identified by respondents. In some cases we engage in further user-centered assessment to gain a better understanding of the user experience as we work towards solutions. We also consult and check back through various means with users to ensure we are addressing identified problems. Assessment is included in all roles within the libraries and assessment involving users may be conducted by individuals or groups of staff across the libraries, e.g., web usability is addressed by the Web Services Librarian and the committee he leads whereas other assessment may be carried out by library directors and staff regarding local issues/problems, and the teaching/liaising librarians gather feedback for improved research support. In all cases, users are a part of assessment and the user voice is heard.

USER EXPERIENCE STAFF

This section examines how your library deploys staff to assess and design the user experience. Some libraries have created specific positions and departments to lead these efforts. Other libraries perform these tasks with staff who have multiple job responsibilities in addition to user experience.

4. What is the position title of the individual in your library who has primary responsibility for coordinating user experience activities? N=68

5. What is the position title of the manager to whom this person reports? N=65

Position Title	Reports to	Comments
Assessment Coordinator; and Instruction & Outreach Librarian	Assessment Coordinator reports to the Executive Associate Director and the Instruction & Outreach Librarian reports to the Head of Instruction Services.	
Assessment & Planning Librarian	AUL for Collections and Services	The Assessment & Planning Librarian has primary responsibilities, but several other staff from various departments are routinely involved in these efforts. The Assessment & Planning Librarian reports to the AUL for C&S.
Assessment Coordinator	Associate Dean for Organizational Development	Actually, the Assessment Coordinator has primary responsibility for user feedback and then distributes that to the appropriate staff to figure out how to address user needs and experience. Other areas, such as Access Services, Subject Librarians, and departmental libraries, have responsibility for user experience and report to other AD's.
Assessment Director	Head of Access Services and Assessment	Although the Assessment Director coordinates library assessment activities, many departments and staff have responsibility for conducting assessments and user experience activities.
Assessment Librarian	University Librarian	
Assessment Librarian	Associate University Librarian	
Assessment Librarian, and Communications Librarian	Both report directly to the Dean of Libraries.	These two librarians work together to implement user experience activity.
Assistant Dean (Client Services)	Associate Dean	This is a new position, established in October 2010, to which all the branch and unit heads report.
Assistant Dean for User Services	Dean of Libraries	We also have a newly formed assessment council made up of library staff and until recently we had an officer for assessment (.5 FTE). The Assistant Dean for Collections and Scholar Services and the Head of Spencer Research Library are also involved in assessment activities within their respective areas.
Assistant University Librarian, Outreach and Academic Services	University Librarian	

Position Title	Reports to	Comments
Associate Dean	Dean	We haven't really had anyone coordinating them in the past, but we have recently hired a new associate dean who has much more interest in increasing efforts in this area.
Associate Dean	Dean	But I get help from many folks: we have an Assessment Team and an Assessment Team Leader. We have a Data Officer and lots of volunteer public services librarians for these projects.
Associate Dean for Assessment, Personnel & Research	Dean	We have an Assessment Team which is led by a Reference/Outreach Librarian.
Associate Dean for Information Services	Dean	User experience tasks are primarily a function of public services.
Associate Dean for Research and Learning Services	Dean of the Marriott Library and University Librarian	With the assistance of the Budget and Planning Director and other Associate Deans.
Associate Dean of Library Services; Associate Dean of Library Services and Director of the Health Sciences Library	Dean and University Librarian	Two Associate Deans share the oversight responsibility.
Associate Director for Public Services	Director of Libraries	
Associate University Librarian for Collections and User Services	University Librarian	We have a distributed system with respect to user experience activities. While our AUL for Collections and User Services has primary responsibility, other groups also actively lead projects. I would include both our Associate University Librarian for Information Technology and our Director, Academic Technology and Instructional Services, as holding key roles in this area.
Associate University Librarian for Graduate & Research Services	University Librarian	
Associate University Librarian for Planning and Organizational Research	Vice President for Information Services and University Librarian	The work is shared with the Associate University Librarian for Research and Instructional Services and the Digital User Services Librarian, for which we are currently recruiting. The Digital User Services Librarian reports to the Associate University Librarian for Research and Instructional Services.
Associate University Librarian for Services	University Librarian	

Position Title	Reports to	Comments
Associate University Librarian, Information Services		This position has oversight for the reference department, branch libraries, circulation department, and the map and sound and moving image libraries.
AUL for Public Services	University Librarian	
AUL for Research and Instructional Services	Dean of the Library	At this time we are not really giving any one staff member primary responsibility for this although the AUL is working to lead the effort. The goal is to engage as many public service staff as possible and have them believing that they all (each one) are responsible for UX activity. At different times, different staff, be they department heads, access service clerks or reference librarians, can be leading some part of the activity.
Coordinator, Information Literacy and Assessment	Director of Libraries	The title is fluid, as we are in the process of reorganizing. After the reorganization, this position will report to the newly created Head of Discovery and Delivery Services.
Coordinator of Training and Assessment	Associate Dean of Libraries for Finance, Administration, and Human Resources	This is a new position (began November 2010).
Decision Support Analyst (DSA)	Associate University Librarian for User Services	
Development, Assessment, and Marketing Librarian	Associate University Librarian (Access)	
Director of Access, Information, and Research Services	Deputy University Librarian	
Director of Anthropological Research	Vice Provost and Dean of the Libraries	
Director of Assessment	Associate University Librarian, Organizational Development	
Director of Assessment	Associate University Librarian for Public Services	
Director of Education and Volunteer Programs	Director of Museum Programs	The Director of Museum Programs currently reports to the Assistant Archivist with oversight of all archival related programs in the Washington, DC area.
Director of Planning Assessment and Organizational Effectiveness	Dean of University Libraries	This is a newly recreated position. We're still exploring the scope and scale of responsibilities.

Position Title	Reports to	Comments
Director of Planning, Assessment, and Research	University Librarian	Public Services division also has significant responsibilities related to user experience design and assessment.
Director of Project Management and Assessment	Associate Dean of the University Libraries	We are in the process of finalizing an assessment plan, developed in collaboration with team leaders (department head equivalents) that will guide our activities over the next 3 to 5 years.
Director of Public Relations	Dean of Libraries	At this time, the library does not have a designated position, but coordination of much outreach and assessment of those efforts falls to the above position.
Director, Assessment and Planning	Senior Associate Dean of Libraries	This position provides support and coordination as needed but user experience activities occur throughout the organization and often are led by those individuals and/or groups closest to the specific issue. For example, usability is under the aegis of our Web Services person.
Director, Partnerships and Outreach Programs	Associate Librarian for Library Services	
Director, User Experience	Associate Dean for Library Technologies	
Faculty Director for Library Information Technology	Associate Director for Administrative Services	Even though we list this position, there is not much of a coordinated effort. This is mostly project-based for us.
First Year Experience Librarian	Head, Instructional Services	Yes, the effort is shared. The FYE Librarian leads the effort for freshmen and for undergraduates more broadly.
Head Library Learning Services	Associate Dean of University Park Libraries	
Head of Collection Management	Associate Director for Library Services and Collections	
Head of the User Experience Department	Associate University Librarian for Library Information Technology	
Head of UX office	AUL for Public Services	The head of the UX office was formerly the bibliographer for Physics, Math, Astronomy, and Statistics, and still performs those duties.

Position Title	Reports to	Comments
Head, Academic Program Services; Branch Library Head; Communications and Publications Officer; Library Director	Directors report to the University Librarian. Other positions report to the Associate University Librarian, User Services.	
Head, Digital User Experience Department	Associate Dean, Library Academic Services (Public Services)	
Head, Music Library	Associate University Librarian for Public Services and Collection Development	The head of the Music Library has dual responsibilities as she also serves as chair of the UX Team. This AUL position is currently in flux. The incumbent left in December. The library is restructuring and has not yet determined how either the AULs or the UX Team will be organized.
Head, User Experience Group	Associate Director for Research & Instructional Services	This is a new position for us, since June 2010. We reorganized the MIT Libraries at that time and created a new department.
Interim Director, Peabody Library (with system-wide assessment responsibilities; title in the works)	Dean of Libraries	
Planning & Assessment Officer	Dean of Libraries	
Research & Assessment Analyst	Director of the Program Management Center	
Student Liaison	Associate University Librarian for Administration, Development, and Human Resources	The Eckles Outreach Coordinator also has responsibility for user experiences at our Mt. Vernon campus. This position reports to Associate University Librarian for Public Services. AUL for Administration, Development, and Human Resources also chairs Assessment Group and meets with the Outreach Group.
User Assessment Librarian	Assistant University Librarian for Scholarly Communications, Personnel & Assessment	Although my title is User Assessment Librarian, I also plan, implement, consult, and collaborate on other assessment activities in the library.
User Engagement Librarian and Assessment Coordinator	Associate Dean	
User Experience Librarian	Head, Discovery & Access	There are two UX librarians and one UX team member who is not a librarian.

Additional Comments

Assessment broadly defined is the purview of the Director for Planning and Communication. As noted above, library user experience activities are more distributed.

No one particular individual who has primary responsibility for coordinating user experience activities.

No one position.

No single position has primary responsibility. In our current organization, the three Associate Vice-Provosts with responsibility for Collections, Learning, and Research Support respectively work collaboratively to coordinate user experience activities. All report to the Vice Provost (Libraries and Cultural Resources and University Librarian).

No such position. We have decentralized with departments and committees responsible for assessment in areas related to their activities. If we want to undertake a library assessment, we use a committee but that committee is currently inactive.

There is no position.

There is no single individual responsible for coordinating user experience activities. This responsibility is distributed among several individuals.

There is not one individual with the primary responsibility for coordinating user experience activities.

There is not one person; it's done on a one-time basis. We have an assessment committee with rotating membership.

We do have someone with the title, "Website Architect and User Experience Analyst" who is responsible for UX in the web environment. Reports to AUL for IT.

We do not have a specific position devoted to "user experience," however, we do have a committee called the "User Feedback and Assessment Committee" that helps with training and support for user experience assessment.

6. **In the matrix below, please indicate which staff in your library participate in assessment and design/implementation of the user experience. Check all that apply. N=70**

	N	Assessment	Design/Implementation
Individual staff from various departments depending on the need at the time	66	64	65
An ad hoc task force or committee	45	43	41
Staff in another department in the library	40	38	39
A standing committee	40	37	34
Assessment librarian	35	34	24
Outside consultant	18	12	13
User Experience librarian	17	16	16
Staff in an autonomous User Experience department in the library	10	9	10
Other individual(s) or group(s)	13	12	12

Please specify the other individual(s) or group(s) and briefly describe their role in user experience activities.

Assessment

Institutional Research Planning.

Design/Implementation

This is highly distributed. For example, we have a Web Development committee whose members conduct usability testing and then implement changes to the website. We have an ad hoc group working with the Assessment Team to analyze our LibQUAL+® data and recommend changes. We have hired outside consultants three times over the last several years to assess particular parts of the organization.

Both

Anthropology professor – collaborated with us on ethnographic studies. Process Improvement Specialist – works closely with anyone in the library doing assessment.

As needed, the Assessment Librarian draws in other experts to advise/assist with assessment projects.

Associate Vice-Provosts working collaboratively and with senior leadership team.

Consulting with staff at the university's Institute for Assessment and Compliance.

Decision support analyst performs a variety of assessments that library administration deems appropriate, and also assists other library groups, committees, or individuals in planning or implementing assessments related to their areas of responsibility.

George Washington University Program Board, University Student Association, Graduate Student Advisory Board, and Faculty Senate Committee on Libraries have various influences upon library services, library space utilization, operating budget, department funds.

Our Executive Council and the other Associate Deans of the Marriott Library (Special Collections, Information Technology Services, Research and Learning Services, and Scholarly Resources and Collections).

Research Librarian for Emerging Technologies and Service Innovation focuses on investigating and implementing new technology initiatives to enhance user experience.

The library has hired a graduate student to specifically focus on assessment activities.

We have an Assessment Interest Group focused on learning more about library assessment and creating a culture of assessment in the libraries. The group helps to inform our assessment program and activities.

Additional Comments

Participation in these activities is dispersed throughout the organization. The Libraries Assessment and Metrics Team is a standing committee that serves as a resource for design/development and assessment activities.

Our Head of Digital Experience Services leads website and discovery related user experience activities. Led by the Head of Digital Experience Services, we have a Web Interfaces Group (WIG) that includes an implementation team. The implementation team is co-led by two user services librarians. Our overall assessment strategy is coordinated by the Head, Assessment and Planning.

Our Reference, Instruction, and Circulation departments are active in assessing user services and we have just formed a library-wide standing assessment committee that will coordinate assessment needs throughout the libraries. Our subject librarians have held periodic focus groups on issues such as moving materials to storage. The Center for Digital Scholarship librarians and staff have established advisory boards for various services.

Staff in the Learning Commons, in particular, help with surveys. For project-based assessment, like usability testing of the library's web tools, interested staff may participate.

Task forces involved in initiatives have conducted their own assessment, e.g., VuFind user groups. Standing committees such as the Information Literacy Committee are involved in assessment of their activities.

Technology and public services staff conduct usability testing. The Dean conducts focus groups. An ad hoc group led the LibQUAL+® survey efforts.

The Coordinator of Training and Assessment will, eventually, be the person primarily responsible for overseeing all assessment activities and for reporting results to stakeholders. Assessment Steering Committee—comprised of individuals throughout the organization and tasked with providing guidance to assessment activities and conducting library-wide assessment as needed User Spaces Task Force—tasked with looking at how library patrons interact with our facilities and making recommendations for improvement. Web Services Coordinator conducts web usability studies and involved representatives from other departments as there is an interest. Strategic Plan Oversight and Implementation Committee indirectly involved in that the Assessment Steering Committee and the User Spaces Task Force report back to this group and SPOIC actually makes recommendations to the dean. Lindsey+Asp is a relatively new partnership but this is a student run public relations agency on-campus that we hope will conduct focus groups with students.

The university's office of institutional research provides support and expertise in assessment activities.

The Virtual Library Group (a standing committee of sorts) has primary responsibility for user experience assessment for virtual spaces and products.

We have a standing usability committee comprised of 5 to 6 librarians who are called up to do usability testing of library websites, software, etc.

We have recently formed a Learning & Assessment Team that is focusing primarily on assessment of our information literacy program.

We use project teams to develop and implement new services and products. These teams are usually responsible for assessing the effectiveness and satisfaction of users as well. We do not have a position designated as user experience librarian. We do have a recently implemented website product management group that has responsibility for usability and assessing effectiveness of the library's website. We have used an outside consultant in the past for usability studies but now rely on trained staff.

Web Librarian: implementation of interface improvements, web usability. Digital Technologies Librarian: implementation of design improvement. Assessment Working Group: plans and implements system-wide assessment projects like LibQUAL+®. Others: as appropriate by project.

USER EXPERIENCE ACTIVITIES

Please select up to two user experience activities the library has recently undertaken that had the biggest impact or were most innovative and answer the following questions about those activities.

7. What broad aspect of the user's library experience was the activity trying to assess and/or design? Check all that apply. N=70

Library facilities (space configuration, navigation)	45	64%
Library services (ILL, reference, instruction, etc.)	37	53%
Library technology (website usability, navigation)	36	51%
Library resources (search and discovery, collections, formats)	35	50%
Other aspect	4	6%

Please describe other aspect.

ClimateQUAL® to assess staff perceptions of their working environment.

Desired outside services (writing center, tutoring, etc.)

Intersection of library services, resources, and facilities with those of archives, museum, and press.

The totality of the library service and physical environment.

8. Please briefly describe the scope of the activity. N=64

A campus-wide investigation of faculty, staff, and student perspectives on the highest priorities for library services and resources, and the importance of various services and resources.

A completely renovated main floor, including information and circulation service points, offices for staff, reference collection, many public seating and work spaces, and a cafe.

A Faculty Library Survey was administered in October 2010. Thirty-two percent of faculty completed the web-based anonymous survey which asked faculty about their use of, and satisfaction with, library resources, services, and facilities.

A paper survey was administered to all users of the Learning Commons during a 24-hour period.

A service quality survey was administered and 3000 faculty and students responded.

A study of undergraduate library use including, but not limited to, input on the redesign of our periodicals room.

A user survey (via SurveyMonkey) was sent to 16,000 library patrons in fall 2010 to measure library performance and user satisfaction with an emphasis on facilities, services, and technological resources.

A work group was formed to investigate developing a Research Commons in the library. Focus groups and a survey were conducted.

At this point we are not talking about UX in the context of a particular service or technology, although we have in the past done usability studies of the OPAC and website. We are more focused on discussing UX in a holistic way. What is the experience we have now and what could it be?

Collections: Library moved to a new approval plan that emphasizes electronic over print as well as print/electronic purchase-on-demand. Users now have greater input on collection decisions.

Comparative usability of discovery tools and next generation catalog interfaces.

Conducted five focus groups targeting various user groups to assess the library's homepage for functionality and usability.

Digital Social Science Center (DSSC) Evaluation: understand the awareness, use of, and service quality of the DSSC, which has been open for 1.5 years. This was primarily done via a questionnaire distributed in-library, and via e-mail to target student groups.

Ethnographic study incorporating 20, one-hour interviews with undergraduate students captured on video.

From December 2008 through to June 2009, Libraries and Cultural Resources conducted a thorough implementation planning exercise in preparation for the opening of a new facility, The Taylor Family Digital Library. Six teams: Collections, Learning Services, Media/Technology, Outreach and Community Involvement, Research Support, and Staffing; included representation from all areas of Libraries and Cultural Resources and all staffing groups. The work was coordinated by a librarian assigned full time to this project in the role of Director, Implementation. All teams included gathering information about the User Experience within their mandate.

In an effort to improve the "way finding" in the library, we observed users, asked them to get from point A to point B in the library and mapped their route, and put up temporary signs and asked for user feedback on their design and content.

In planning and preparing for the Learning Studio, we conducted a wide range of activities to gather user input. This included observational studies, e-mail survey, furniture voting, focus groups, and in-person survey with handheld devices. These focused on the use of space, furniture, and group needs, technology required, and available services desired.

In planning for a major renovation of the first and second floor of the main library, we have been gathering input from our users in formal and informal ways to better inform our planning.

In the spring of 2010, the library ran a LibQUAL+® survey, has already responded to some key concerns raised in the survey regarding library hours, and is developing an action plan to look at other areas.

Last year, a number of librarians and IT staff were charged to create a replacement for WebVoyage, the current OPAC interface. To determine the elements necessary for this new discovery tool, the group identified a group of undergraduate and graduate students, faculty, librarians, and university staff for usability testing of various library catalogs, including the Penn Libraries' new books discovery tool, whose digital library architecture was proven successful and envisioned as a suitable replacement for the current OPAC.

Learning Commons design: Affinity focus groups were set up to ask undergraduates: "How would you design or imagine the learning space for your ideal academic learning environment?" Students were given post-it notes and grouped their ideas based on themes. Design charettes were used.

LibQUAL+®.

LibQUAL+® 2010 survey: campus-wide, Vancouver campus. The UBC Okanagan campus conducted its own LibQUAL+® survey.

LibQUAL+® 2009 survey.

LibQUAL+® Lite.

LibQUAL+® Lite, Canadian national edition.

LibQUAL+® survey. "LibQUAL+® is a suite of services that libraries use to solicit, track, understand, and act upon users' opinions of service quality."

Library Live is an all-day conference for faculty and graduate students highlighting information resources, tools, and services.

Library services: two combined studies looking at building use, activities engaged in while in the building (survey and unobtrusive observation), and a reference question analysis project.

Overhaul and redesign of library's website.

Re-envisioning first floor as student-centered, collaborative spaces that offer rich technologies and high quality services from the libraries and several university partners.

Redesigning the old computer lab from rows of computers to include modern collaborative spaces while maintaining individual workstations. Redesigning study rooms.

Renovation of a branch library.

Single Search Box Usability Testing: users were asked to search for an item on the website or in a database using a single search box.

Studied use of various reference services. Analyzed categories of questions asked at the desk (notes are kept in online database) and through virtual services. Satisfaction survey/feedback form was redesigned and linked from these services. Services are currently undergoing a redesign based on the results. Partially related to this was a study of how students use the physical spaces in the central library including the main information desk.

Student Advisory board and an ad hoc provost-formed student group with library and university staff are gathering ideas for the renovation of the 1st floor, long wished for, partially planned, but not definitely funded. Now that the university has agreed and has hired an architect, the planning is moving along quickly.

Survey to assess instruction.

The concept for Patron for a Day (PFAD) was generated in one of the first meetings of the User Experience group. The discussion focused on how empathy is a key ingredient in "design thinking" and we wanted to find a way to help our staff build empathy for our users. Technically speaking, PFAD is a collection of three different tests, taken by staff volunteers at one of our four different locations. Practically speaking, it is an opportunity for staff to learn what it is like to be a user by performing a series of tasks patrons regularly perform in our physical spaces. While designing a series of tests to develop empathy, we realized we were also designing usability tests of our physical spaces. Some tasks required interaction with technology, such as scanners and computers, while others just required interaction with the physical space and collections. Some tasks were easy – "find the restroom;" others were harder – "scan pages from book X and send to your e-mail." In most cases, staff members visited libraries they were less familiar with to complete their "test." They were asked to take notes about their experience (good and bad) and, after completion, were asked to rate each task and enter their comments into an established web form. We had twenty volunteers complete one of three different tests at one of four locations.

The concept for the University of Washington Libraries Research Commons came out of the Libraries' desire to respond to the evolving research and collaborative needs of student and faculty. The growth of data-driven research, digital scholarship, and interdisciplinary studies required a re-examination of services and physical spaces being provided for our community. The consolidation of print collections and service points at the UW Libraries, in response to budget reductions and trends away from physical collection use, left the ground floor of the Allen South Library available for renovation in late 2009. A Research Commons Planning Committee reviewed the literature on information commons within academic libraries, examined library digital commons, and conducted interviews and surveys with faculty, staff, and students around campus to identify service gaps and departmental research needs. In doing so, a set of needs emerged that informed their final recommendation on services and resources to be offered in the future UW Libraries Research Commons space. A report from the UW Learning and Scholarly Technologies group on their extensive study of UW student learning space needs was also examined in planning for the space. A design firm was hired in early 2010 and, utilizing data from both of these sources, they developed an initial plan for the space and followed this with a design charette conducted with library staff, students, and faculty to get more feedback. Assessment was an integral part of the initial design of the research commons, and comes out of the Libraries' ongoing assessment program. The design and construction of the Research Commons was completed in October, and the space opened at the start of Autumn Quarter 2010. Once open, assessment was conducted through regular observation of user activity in the Research Commons. In late February 2011, we began conducting strategic discussion groups with users of the Research Commons to find out how the space, furnishings, equipment, and services have been utilized. The results of these discussion groups will help inform the development an in-libraries use survey for Research Commons users, to be distributed in Spring Quarter 2011.

The design and implementation of a new online credit-bearing course: Research Lab. The project involved collaboration with the English department to identify learning goals, development of the online course including content, offering the course for the first time, and assessing the student experience through use of a local Teacher Course Evaluation tool, other feedback from students, and feedback from instructors in the English department.

The goal of the South Reading Room research project was to determine how the main library reading room could be improved the meet users' needs. The project had three components: observations, then focus groups, followed by a survey. Subsequent to the formal study, alternative types of furniture were brought in for users to indicate their preferences.

The goal was to launch a new search and discovery unified interface for the online catalog and the digital library.

The library conducts an annual survey, which surveys graduate students, undergraduates, and faculty in rotation on a three-year cycle. The survey is intended to gauge user experiences and needs with regard to collections, services, and both virtual and physical spaces.

The library recently completed a redesign of the entire library website and catalog. Users were involved throughout the process.

The library recently renovated a commons space, primarily relying on input about furnishings, aesthetics, layout, and design ideas from students. After the space opened in fall 2009, the User Experience department and Associate Dean for Public Services began an effort to determine how well the space was meeting student needs using a survey instrument that included both quantitative satisfaction measures, as well as open-ended qualitative comments.

The library was opening up a new space in a building on campus. A small-scale ethnographic project was undertaken to access user needs for that space.

The Music Library Space Use Study was set up to investigate low scores and accompanying comments from a LibQUAL+® survey that identified space as a problem by all three user groups in the Music Library. Western Libraries conducted a Music Library Space Use Study in two phases: first, an observation study and then later, in phase 2, interviews.

The scope was to answer the following questions: Who are the current visitors? What were visitors' general reactions to the Library of Congress? Are visitors' expectations being met? Why? What types of experiences did visitors take advantage of at the Library of Congress? How do visitors perceive the Library of Congress compared to other DC cultural attractions?

The survey was used to assess the frequency of utilization and satisfaction level with the library's resources—including computers, audio-visual equipment, databases, and printers—and its services such as instruction, information or reference, interlibrary loan, and circulation.

The User Spaces Task Force created a survey to poll users on how they interact with the libraries facilities, what improvements they would like to see, and the considerations made when choosing where to study within the library.

This study employed methods of user feedback collection to learn about the information needs of sciences faculty and students at the University of North Carolina at Chapel Hill in order to improve library services for this population. Our research questions we were attempting to address were: What are the information needs and behaviors of faculty and students in the sciences at UNC-Chapel Hill? How can the UNC libraries best meet those needs through the provision of resources and services?

To learn how users navigated our Digital Collections website and how they used the search options.

Upon the launch of a re-designed website, we mounted a feedback survey and conducted usability testing.

Usability testing for redesign of library website.

User-centered website redesign.

Way finding Exercise: We conducted three way finding studies with a total of 10 participants covering three distinct areas of a single library building. Each participant performed at least 10 tasks over the course of one hour. For each task a printout of a preselected OPAC item record was given to the participant, who then had to attempt to locate the item on the shelf while the facilitator observed. Participants were also asked to locate amenities such as bathrooms and copy machines, and completed a survey following the tasks.

We administer LibQUAL+® every two years to capture user perceptions on library service quality, by asking questions in three "dimensions": Affect of Service, Library as Place, and Information Control. Survey results provide a snapshot of user perceptions of service levels (minimally-acceptable, desired, and perceived) at a particular point in time.

We administered LibQUAL+® in fall 2010 for the first time. We also surveyed faculty for their rating of liaison services. We routinely assess instruction. Other recent surveys include MINES® and ClimateQUAL®.

We conducted a series of observations (remotely) with students conducting research for a class assignment to see how they used library resources (or not!) in an unmediated setting. We did not identify ourselves as the library so as to not influence their behavior. We've completed a pilot phase and have plans to expand it in the fall.

We conducted an ethnographic research study using surveys and interviews to study how undergraduate and graduate students and faculty were using the existing Rutgers University Libraries Web interface to conduct online research and compose papers and reports.

We examined the use of our central search and discovery interface that resides on our library home page. Currently, we use a tabbed system where the user must select which tool they want to use, such as the catalog, e-journals, databases, or article search. The goal was to determine which tabs were seen as most useful, as well as whether the presence or number of tabs was confusing. A second project was spawned in which we investigated the use and effectiveness of our federated articles search interface. This included looking at use statistics as well as user interviews. For both studies we used Morae software, filmed the participants, and presented results to the larger library community.

We recently completed a two-part web UX study: one on performance support needs and another on conceptualizing web space in general.

We undertook a two-year study of how undergraduates do their work. We had a number of sub groups that specifically looked at services, technology, and facilities.

We were gathering user feedback to proposed plans for the renovation of a particular, subject library.

9. **Is the target of the activity any typical library user or a specific category of user (e.g., faculty, graduate students, etc.)? N=70**

Any user	39	56%
A specific category of user	31	44%

If you answered "A specific category of user," please identify the category.

Educators, primarily, and their students.

Faculty.

Faculty and graduate students.

Faculty and students in the sciences.

Faculty, graduate students, and undergraduate students of the Don Wright Faculty of Music.

Faculty, staff, students; the project did not include community users.

For the pilot phase, we focused on undergraduate students in humanities. Prior experience using the library was not required.

Graduate and undergraduate students, teaching assistants and faculty.

Graduate students.

Last year we surveyed graduate and professional students; this year we're surveying undergraduates, and next year we'll survey faculty. We'll continue to survey each population in rotation in a three-year cycle.

LibQUAL+® and MINES® included all users, while other assessment tools targeted faculty (liaison survey), staff (ClimateQUAL®), and students (instructional assessment).

Primarily undergraduate students.

Social Science graduate students and library users.

Students (undergraduate or graduate).

Students using the newly renovated 2nd floor West Commons area.

The focus is ASU faculty, staff and students.

Undergraduate students.

Undergraduate students.

Undergraduate students.

Undergraduate students, graduate students.

Undergraduate students taking English 102 courses (a required General Education class).

Undergraduate students, graduate students, faculty.

Undergraduate students, primarily lower-division.

Undergraduate, graduate, and faculty.

Undergraduates.

Undergraduates.

Undergraduates, graduate students, faculty.

Undergraduates, graduates, and faculty.

Usability was conducted with students, primarily. The feedback survey was open to all.

Users of the Learning Commons.

We've done both. Some efforts have been open to the entire community; other projects have targeted a particular group, such as graduate students, or ENGL 101 class instructors, etc.

10. **What is the source of funding for this activity? Check all that apply. N=70**

Library operating budget	61	87%
Special one-time funds	10	14%
Grant	3	4%
Other	13	19%

Please describe other source of funding.

Campus funded as part of a campus strategic planning taskforce.

Campus Operations (facilities) supplemented library gift funds to implement the improvements.

Collections – use collections budget.

Foundation funds for survey incentives (donuts).

Gift money.

Kresge Challenge Grant.

MINES® was paid for by the Controller's Office.

Most of the monies are being raised from private donors.

No funds were used; staff on that floor managed the collection and analysis.

No special funding need.

Special one-time funds came from the Office of the Provost; "other" funding came from endowments.

The Foundation for the National Archives raised private funds for the project.

University and fund raising.

ASSESSING THE USER EXPERIENCE

11. What tool(s) did/will your library use to evaluate or inform the user experience? Check all that apply. N=70

Surveys	56	80%
Focus groups	39	56%
Anecdotal comments	29	41%
Suggestion box (physical or online)	25	36%
Usability testing	25	36%
E-mail	24	34%
Social media	18	26%
Design charrettes	15	22%
Furniture trials	13	19%
Instruction session evaluations	13	19%
Online discussion forums/message boards	8	12%
Video diaries	3	4%
Audio diaries	2	3%
Other tool(s)	29	41%

Please specify other tool(s).

Annual statistics on circulation, gate counts, reference and instruction.

Database recording of all reference transactions: type coded by categories, mode of transaction, date and time.

Earlier LibQUAL+® survey comments.

Ethnographic observational studies.

Ethnographic research.

Faculty interviews. Online card sorting.

Had a revolving question of the day on our website asking questions about user experience.

Individual way finding sessions (usability for the physical building).

Interviews.

Interviews, mapping exercise, photo diary.

Mapping diaries, interviews, photo diaries.

Notes and photographs.

Observation survey tool with 52 variables completed by researchers. Interview survey tool. Interviews were audio-taped and researchers took notes during the interviews. Audio-tapes were later transcribed.

Observations.

One-on-one interviews with a consulting anthropologist.

Photo diaries, day mapping, print diaries.

Regular staff observation of space use.

Remote observation.

Student Advisory Group input. Student interns.

This project is not geared toward assessment of a particular service or technology, but is instead focused on helping us to better understand what our UX is and could be.

University of Arizona Teacher Course Evaluation tool and assessment of student learning comparing student competency at the beginning and the end of the course and comparing the abilities of students who took the course to students who did not take the course.

Unobtrusive observation; reference question analysis; Plus Delta.

User interviews were used to develop composite personas that guided user-centered discussions about information architecture and design. Also used an anthropological approach of going to dormitories and observing students as they searched for information.

Videotaped interviews; LibQUAL+®; flip charts with questions and users were asked to write down their answers; consultation with the Library Student Advisory Group; survey tours with photographs.

We conducted focus groups prior to the survey to identify marketing strategies and to raise awareness of the survey and gain support prior to the launch.

We created a Ning called "Collaborate" through which we continually talked with our target audience throughout design and development.

We have used several methods to gather input from our users regarding the renovation. We used white boards placed throughout the library asking various open-ended questions about the renovation. We collected over 1000 comments that were analyzed. Also as part of a class project, students from a graphics design class analyzed the way-finding aspects of the building by observing students who were roaming the stacks looking for items. The students prepared a formal report and presentation outlining their findings and recommendations in the following four areas: signage, interior design, communication points, and maps & floor plans.

We used Morae software to record and analyze the user interviews which captured video and audio of users in process.

Worked with a design engineering class. The renovation was the focus of one of their projects. Individual interviews.

12. **Did/will your library send a direct invitation to potential participants or have an open recruitment of library users to participate in this activity or use both methods to recruit participants? N=69**

Open recruitment	18	26%
Direct invitation	14	20%
Both	37	54%

13. **What tools or outlets did/will your library use to recruit library users to participate in this activity? Check all that apply. N=69**

E-mail	49	71%
Library web page	42	61%
User contact from subject specialist/faculty liaisons/bibliographers	41	59%
Posters and/or flyers	36	52%
Social media	19	28%
Giveaways (bookmarks, pens, pencils, etc.)	18	26%
Campus media (newspaper, radio, TV)	18	26%
In-house media (library newsletters, for example)	17	25%
Cover letter attached to survey	15	22%
Local media (newspapers, radio, TV)	2	3%
Other	15	22%

Please specify other tool or outlet.

Announcements to Senate members and Senate Committee members. The current Assessment Librarian is the elected librarians' representative to Senate through 2011.

As we receive critical feedback from users, we typically contact them after we have attempted to improve some issue they addressed. We will invite them to serve as usability test or focus group participants.

Asked for participation by users in the reading room. Graduate student project leader invited classmates to participate.

Electronic signage.

Faculty of Music meetings with all user groups, undergraduate student newsletter in the Faculty of Music.

On-the-spot questions to students in the user spaces.

Partnered with administrators in other units of the university.

Recruited users in the building.

The Library Executive contacted faculty members and team members contacted students.

Those who volunteered after filling out our annual user satisfaction survey.

Used students to recruit participants.

User contact from campus academic advising unit.

Visitor interception at strategic locations throughout the library.

We surveyed every person who left the library during pre-defined times. We recorded every reference question asked.

14. Did/will your library offer any type of incentive to encourage users to participate in the activity? N=68

Yes	50	73%
No	18	27%

If yes, please indicate the type of incentive. Check all that apply. N=51

Food, drink, and/or candy	31	61%
Gift cards	26	51%
Cash payment	3	6%
Other prize or incentive	11	22%

Please specify other prize of incentive.

Apparel from the university bookstore.

Bookmark or a DVD with interactive games.

Donation to the local food bank for every survey received.

Drawing for a gift card to a local business.

iPad.

MacBooks and iPods — one each for the undergraduate and graduate student categories.

Nooks.

Pizza works with students!

$20 gift card from campus bookstore, + food service for each 1-hour session.

Thumb drive.

We offered a hand written thank you, and a small token card to the campus coffee shop.

We offered prizes that were donated by local businesses. We also made a small donation to a local food bank for each survey response.

SHARING THE ASSESSMENT RESULTS

15. Did/will the library share the results of the assessment with others (funding/governing boards, users, etc.)? N=69

Yes	58	84%
No	11	16%

If yes, please briefly describe to whom the results are communicated, the method(s) used, and whether the communication method varies by audience.

A written final report was shared with the Library (leadership) Council as well as with Campus Operations. This led to partial funding to implement the recommendations. An executive summary appeared in our Library Annual Report that was shared with campus leadership, donors, etc.

A written summary of results was shared with the in-house Content DM Administrators Group which is responsible for the content on our Digital Collections website. A presentation about the project was given to the Assessment Team and there was brief write-up about the assessment in the staff newsletter.

ALA poster session (poster), library employees (presentations in meetings), university library committee (presentation).

Campus community and campus leadership: communicated through written reports.

Comments obtained through interviews with faculty members were summarized in a Strategic Planning Report created by the architects. The report was shared with a University Space Planning Committee.

Conference presentations (IUG, ALA Annual, and possibly IFLA) as well as an intended article for *Library Trends*.

Data is used in budget presentations to the President's Executive Team; data is also presented to staff. Method varies by audience.

Depending on the assessment it will be shared with users and stakeholders at open meetings or internally through sharing reports.

Faculty Senate Library Committee Council of Academic Deans Libraries' Faculty and Staff Professional Presentations IT Administrators.

Final reports completed by each team and an executive report summarizing most important recommendations written by team chairs in collaboration with Director, Implementation. Reports posted on Libraries and Cultural Resources web pages and shared with key stakeholders. Teams all provided formal report-back sessions to staff in Libraries and Cultural Resources. Learning Services team shared findings in a presentation to the 5th Canadian Learning Commons Conference.

Hard to answer this question. Some of the results will be directly communicated with the public (we have a "We Heard You" poster campaign every couple of years to highlight what we've changed based on LibQUAL+® results, we have written reports of the results, in some cases, we've written articles about the various projects). We don't have to file a report on the activity with a particular office.

Information on the decision-making process and design has been shared broadly throughout the university and governing board.

Information was shared with library staff, colleges, students union, as well as other libraries. This information was shared via meetings and will also be communicated on the library website.

Institutional Research Planning with a report and PowerPoint, if needed.

Library Administrative Council received a full written, as well as oral, report. All library employees received a brief oral report at a Town Meeting. The study report is posted on our intranet where anyone employed by the library can access the full report.

Library Development Advisory Board, Library Renovation Committee, University Faculty Senate Library Committee will be kept informed and/or assessed for ideas by use of meetings, e-mail, correspondence, and possibly videos or CD-ROMs.

Library management council: presentation and written report.

Library of Congress Executive Committee and Management.

Library staff and advisory committee by direct presentation. Results placed in institutional repository for public access.

Library staff, faculty, Deans, Provost, library supporters.

Other institutions have requested information via e-mail. Library administration: via paper report and presentations. Library staff: via presentations at town hall and other group meetings. Development team working on the user interface: via reports and meetings.

Plans are underway to share results via our website and Facebook site.

Presentation of results at professional conferences.

Public website, Annual Report of the University Librarian to Senate, library advisory committees, Planning & Institutional Research (President's Office), newsletters.

Report is posted on the website/blog. Presentations on campus and at professional meetings.

Reports to the Foundation Board, internal agency reports, using Twitter when new activities are created, alerting workshop participants, etc.

Results are available to library staff in narrative and quantitative form, collected on the Penn library staff web. Results have also been communicated at department head and administrative meetings, as well as public services meetings and forums open to all staff. There is some discussion about publishing the results more broadly, e.g., in an academic article.

Results are communicated to the appropriate user group.

Results are used internally after review by administration. They are e-mailed directly to those who may find them of interest, or who should take action. They are also then posted to our internal intranet for access by other library staff.

Results have been shared with the library administration for inclusion in planning; Faculty of Music Library Council for information; Faculty of Music space planning committee and architects chosen for building redesign and renovations (Music Library is a part of a larger project). A report will be prepared for posting on the Music Library web page.

Results in the form of written reports for the focus groups and surveys were shared with library administrative team and ultimately posted to internal library website for any interested library staff to view. Results were also shared by the Graduate School representative to interested parties in the graduate school administration and by the IT representative to interested parties in the campus IT administration.

Results of the usability testing and survey were shared with the Web Development Committee and the Associate Deans.

Results often show up on our suggestion board but mostly from the results of our efforts, i.e., new lab and new study rooms.

Results shared with Libraries administration and campus administration in report and proposal formats.

Results were communicated to library staff through public meetings and documents posted on the staff intranet.

Shared internally with all relevant committees, who were asked for response reports, posted on our staff web pages for everyone internally and externally to read, shared with our Libraries Advisory Committee of teaching faculty, and included in our annual report.

So far we have shared this only internally with other library departments, but we plan to publish something about it later and perhaps speak at a conference.

Some results were communicated to users via e-mail feedback and a publicly accessible blog. Results were shared with library professionals through conference presentations and published articles.

Studying Students: The Undergraduate Research Project at the University of Rochester.

Summary results were shared with participants in the focus groups (faculty, staff, and students). Communication methods varied: information was posted on the library's website; story in the student newspaper; presentations at departmental/faculty meetings/staff meetings.

The Learning Commons design process was mentioned in the annual report and in the faculty newsletter. The story of the Learning Commons has been communicated to donors by the York Foundation. Internal to York media (YFile) has posted stories on the learning commons.

The related graduate school departments. The results will also be presented at various library meetings and conferences.

The results (including actions taken in response to the results) are posted to the library's web page, shared with those who took the survey, and communicated to all library staff, the Library Board (composed of faculty), and the Library Student Resource Group (advisory group of students).

The results are communicated to the advisory board, library leadership, campus leaders, and at the ARL Assessment Conference.

The results have been communicated to the University of Arizona Provost (in-person presentation), to affected instructors in the English Department, the UA Deans Council (in-person presentation), to the library at large (via e-mail), and to the broader academic library community (through conference presentations).

The results of the assessment are communicated to the most senior levels of the university administration via the library's annual report.

The results were shared with all library staff via our internal website and via e-mail. The results were also shared with the Campus Renovation Committee and the University Committee on Libraries. We also shared the results of the white board comments with students on our large screen monitor display.

The survey results were shared with the Dean and University Librarian, the library staff, the Provost, the funding/governing board, library users and planners in the University Architect's Office. Communication methods varied and were targeted to the audience. We prepared both PowerPoints and summary documents. We had open forum meetings with a presentation and a question and answer segment. At times, only specific data was shared with an individual that was relevant to the topic at hand.

The University Librarian will present the Faculty Library Survey Report to the Provost. After that the report will be distributed to deans, faculty, and library staff. Customized reports will be disseminated as appropriate. All dissemination will be electronic.

Through the design program, press releases, and tours with campus administration, we shared the outcomes and the student input with the entire campus in some form or another.

To user community on our website, through faculty advisory committee, through subject liaisons, to Provost, Chancellor and other deans personally.

We did get IRB approval for this study, but the results were only shared internally with the librarians that work in the new space, the head of reference, and the executive team of the library.

We gave a presentation to staff to share results and discuss findings. Next we will post our final report to our public website and shared via the staff intranet. We'll also be holding a series of discussions with staff who are interested in continuing this work and/or incorporating it into another research project.

We have shared the results with Lindsey+Asp as they prepare a PR campaign for us.

We presented the results of both studies to the library community at large. The data and presentations are posted on our library website.

We shared the results with the Provost and incorporated our findings into a larger self-study written for a task force examining potential cost savings due to anticipated budget cuts.

While this project was not really an assessment, we are sharing our work with the library staff and administration. We report on it at all-staff meetings and we recently started a blog where we are sharing ideas and information about the library experience.

DESIGN CHANGES

16. Please briefly describe any design changes that have been/will be made based on this user experience activity. N=63

A few minor enhancements will be incorporated into our website design but most of the more complex findings/recommendations will be incorporated into our next large-scale redesign. Many librarians who do instruction reported that the findings have greatly influenced how they will now approach how they teach citation management and advanced search techniques (among other things).

A new Undergraduate Learning Commons is being built adjacent to the library. The commons spaces will include many similar features found in the 2nd floor west space. Furthermore, the approach to evaluating the success of this space will be based on the approach taken for evaluating the library's 2nd floor west commons.

Allocation of graduate study spaces; redesigned learning commons space (Woodward Library); website/access improvements. Underway: a follow up survey on graduate student space/equipment needs for Faculty of Arts users; a follow up inventory of "hidden" collections is in progress to improve access. Student learning activities are being documented in a more systematic way through Desk Tracker. A reference service assessment is underway to identify reference activity in a more detailed way (Desk Tracker).

As a result of feedback gained from the surveys, the library has upgraded computer resources and made physical improvements to the facility, including new seating, retiled floors, and the addition of vibrant artwork throughout the main library.

Based on the results of the survey, the Assessment Committee has identified six areas that will be addressed programmatically.

Changed configuration of new reading room. Added Mac classroom. Glass-walled rooms. Furniture choices.

Changed how the service is staffed. We are looking to purchase management software based on the high number of referrals. We are developing a new training and certification program based on results. We are responding to dissatisfaction expressed with a new management structure and unified services (previously dispersed.)

Changed placement and labeling of search tools on web page. Additional explanatory page on different searches.

Collections: print/electronic purchase-on-demand is impacting how the collections budget will be allocated in the future.

Computer lab: collaborative spaces; better lighting; more electrical outlets; comfortable furniture; added software; more computers, specifically laptops and Macs. Study rooms: increased number of rooms; glass wall to increase light and openness; added some color; new carpet; comfortable furniture; white boards; better lighting; several rooms have technology for group project preparation; added two group film viewing rooms; two small classrooms; several rooms now accommodate 8 to 12 users.

Created a Web Board responsible for a total website redesign and rebuild; other user comments have been woven into goals for other service improvements.

Currently in planning stages of a complete building redesign and renovation to meet the needs of the Faculty of Music, a faculty with a growing student base, both undergraduate and graduate. The results of the Music Library Space Use study are being taken seriously by the architects. It is, however, too soon to say what the changes will be for the Music Library.

Design plans changed, e.g., we added more enclosed group study rooms; decreased amount of lounge furniture, increased number of traditional carrels and small tables; allowed for more collection space so that more of the collection remained on open stacks as opposed to in storage.

Hours of opening for one of the branches have changed and potential changes of hours of opening are being considered for other branches. E-mail notification prior to items being due was instituted. Better coordination of borrower services is being looked at. Resource discovery layer is being looked at. Changes to physical space to improve study areas.

Improved remote access. More online journals. Improved signage. More quiet study areas. New library catalog.

Improvements to signage and documentation in our physical spaces are underway. Larger changes involving creating a more uniform experience for all libraries on campus are under discussion.

Informed redesign of components of library website, as well as space and services in Undergraduate Library.

Initial renovation to develop the Research Commons included the addition of whiteboard walls and tables, rolling chairs, and large plasma screens for collaborative work. A new open presentation place provides an area for research presentations, research skills, and grant writing workshops. Campus partner organizations, including writing centers and the UW Center for Commercialization, provide drop-in office hours in the space. The Research Commons increased UW Seattle Libraries reserveable areas for collaborative work 22%, and has been utilized to leverage partnerships with other organizations on campus and thus provide support on issues of copyright, commercialization of research, grant writing, and media literacy. Current assessment, including focus groups, surveys, and consultation with the Research Commons Advisory board, will inform design changes going forward.

Input from attendees influences our service and resource offerings.

It was determined what services to offer in the space, what hours of staffing would be best, and when to offer classes.

Libraries' main website was redesigned, streamlining search, discovery, and access process, and promoting core user tasks as identified through user testing and feedback.

Made some changes to the interface. For example, we increased the font size of search box labels.

Minor adjustments in library building hours and ILL staffing.

New signs will be put in place this summer to help with navigation in the library.

No specific design changes have been made yet. The purpose of the study was to help us understand the needs of our science faculty and students. Collected data will help inform future decisions about our services and collections for these users.

None yet, but I am hoping we'll use our work to fix things that are broken, be they processes, workflows, physical items, or relationships with the user community.

Not yet known.

Our renovation has been put on hold, unfortunately, but the results have made us rethink some of our current thinking regarding the renovation. Once the renovation begins, there will be many design changes based on the input we gathered. We have made some modifications including changing the design of our floor maps based on the recommendation of the students in the graphic design class.

Over the past few years, we've done a number of large and small redesigns of our web page ("digital branch"). We've made changes in our facilities based on focus group feedback (technology in group study rooms, adding power strips to areas to facilitate laptop use with older furniture, etc.)

Physical signage throughout the building was updated, with many new signs made to address the buildings and the user perspective. Additionally, the project caused us to review all language used in the OPAC to describe the physical locations of materials, all of which will be streamlined, updated and made more uniform.

Radically re-envisioned and re-modeled spaces.

Reassignment of some spaces in our multimedia area to accommodate class viewing of feature film. Provided additional evidence to increase urgency of redesign of web presence. Reorganization influenced by findings, especially the need to reorganize expert staff to better support the research enterprise. Helped clarify for staff how the newly designed facility will support new approaches to learning and research. Access Services and Reference Service workflows are in the process of being redesigned to improve the user experience.

Redesign of the website.

Relevant, effective changes to previous design and structure; more user-friendly interface; more logical arrangement of information for audience.

Renovation of main library facility, including student study areas and a cafe.

Results have been used to support renovations and improvements to physical facilities, the acquisition of Summon, and the acquisition of an ERMS, as well as to establish usability testing of the website.

Several features of the renovation were based on these activities. Furniture design and noise abatement features are two of the most prominent.

Still analyzing data from this survey.

Subject to available funding, research and analysis is in process to implement some of the results identified in the survey.

Survey results informed facilities changes and helped to address the need for a variety of study spaces for students, including quiet study areas. It resulted in modifications to the library web page and our online access tools. We revised and strengthened our student training program to enhance our students' abilities to provide quality service.

The architect's design of the Learning Commons and colors used were informed by the affinity focus groups, as well as concerns raised in LibQUAL+® 2007. The furniture selection and placement was informed by student feedback.

The course has been revised based on feedback and is being marketed specifically to a group of students (Arizona Assurance students) who have been indentified as specifically needing to acquire information literacy/fluency competencies in order to help them succeed.

The design changes are still in process but will include installing more outlets, adding group study rooms, and additional comfortable seating.

The home page for the Digital Collections website was redesigned to incorporate drop down menus for all browsing categories. Also the Advanced Search feature is now available from the top-level page and there is an example of how to use the wild card feature.

The library has acquired new printers with greater capacity; additional databases and new titles for both reference and general circulation.

The library's website was simplified.

The performance support and web redesign studies resulted in many changes to the website. For example, the homepage was tabbed to reduce visual clutter, a tab highlighting services provided by librarians was created (amongst other things), and a "Haven't found what you're looking for" box was added to the bottom of each page to provide a safety net for users who've dead-ended on the site.

The project began as a complete redesign of the online catalog's user interface. UX activities are ongoing, however, and we are committed to an iterative design process.

The renovation and creation of a 24-hour library space was directly influenced by the results of this study.

There have been several changes made based on the two studies. We reduced the number of tabs as many users reported that they didn't understand the difference between them. We redesigned the entire search resources box on the home page to better highlight the key resources. The investigation of the federated articles search interface resulted in a task force being formed to determine whether we should move to web scale discovery. We are now in the process of implementing Summon based on the decision of this task force.

These assessment activities greatly shaped the design and furniture selections of the first phase of the Learning Studio. It also impacted the need for an expanded cafe and the types of services offered within the studio.

This activity is too recent for changes to be seen. The task force will submit their report and recommendations for action will derive from the report.

Too early yet for this.

User feedback directly affected the development of the new OPAC. User comments and suggestions have led to the development of, for example, specific search facets, the layout of the site, and how search results are displayed.

Users helped clarify terminology, subject groupings, overall design (use fewer words, more graphics), simpler navigation/flatter organization; more prominent search features.

We added 80 new electrical outlets and provided wiring to 36 individual study carrels. We added a few more fixed computers and a print station. We purchased 15 tablet-arm chairs and 10 individual study tables. We decided NOT to install display cases in the room after the focus group participants indicated this was definitely not desired.

We are in the process of conducting further studies of the least used service points (by time and place) to decide whether to close them or to revitalize them.

We expect to alter physical arrangements of reference, circulation, services departments/units and student computer space. We might also relocate the building's public entrances, loading dock, and Starbuck's entrance.

We have changed our performance management system based on the results of ClimateQUAL®. We are in the process of analyzing our LibQUAL+® data.

We have created a new coffee shop, upgraded furniture, changed library borrowing policies, changed collection practices (e.g., purchasing additional e-books), and pursued new services (e.g., consortial borrowing, paging).

We rely on user testing to design any web interface and we will modify programming of search appliances and API s based on testing.

When the economy improves and funding becomes available, work may begin on a Research Commons.

17. **How would you characterize the impact of these changes on the user experience? N=63**

Minor modification(s) to the existing design	25	40%
Major modification(s) to the existing design	15	24%
Complete redesign	12	19%
Other	11	18%

Please describe other impact.

It could be major, but there are some contingencies that will affect the outcome.

More of a mix. Some of the findings still need to be fleshed out more with other studies. Some problems witnessed are too big for any single change to solve, some are pretty quick fixes.

Most of the time we will make modifications, but often we design and test as we go along.

Project began as a complete redesign of the online catalog's user interface. We continue to make modifications based on continuing user feedback, usability studies, and a list of redesign projects that could not be completed before the initial launch of the new interface.

Selected issues that surfaced in the survey and focus groups that could be attended to without additional funding were addressed. However, the original purpose of the activity was to collect data to be used in creating a Research Commons.

The immediate impact is visible in the redesigned/renovated user spaces. Some of the longer-term projects have not been assessed yet because the data gathering is underway now.

This was a new space, so it was great to start from a user-centered services point. As the space develops, we will want to do additional focus groups over time, to make sure that we are still making the mark.

Too early for specifics.

Unknown at this point in time, but we are hopeful we will see improvements.

We are in the process of making decisions based on the feedback collected. The purpose was not to redesign a specific website or service desk, but was to help inform future decisions about library support for the sciences generally.

While we don't have specific examples, LibQUAL+® and ClimateQUAL® have changed the mindset of upper management to be cognizant of how the current environment is negatively impacting the user experience.

If you want to describe a second user experience activity, please continue to the next screen. If not, please click here then click the Next>> button below to jump to the User Groups and Advisory Boards section.

Only one user experience activity to describe. N=19

18. What broad aspect of the user's library experience was the activity trying to assess and/or design? Check all that apply. N=51

Library technology (website usability, navigation)	32	63%
Library facilities (space configuration, navigation)	23	45%
Library services (ILL, reference, instruction, etc.)	20	39%
Library resources (search and discovery, collections, formats)	20	39%
Other aspect	6	12%

Please describe other aspect.

Context, Staff, Equipment.

Gather data on the users of the Info Commons in Langsam Library.

Marketing tool for reference services.

Regular meetings with student governance and advisory boards to assess needs and build support for student fee increases.

The role of the libraries and readiness to partner in support of new forms of digital scholarship in the humanities.

19. Please briefly describe the scope of the activity. N=50

A librarian and a member of the Center for Instructional Technology did an intensive study on the Cultural Anthropology department. They employed methods used at the University of Minnesota to interview each individual faculty member. They also held focus groups with graduate students. The goal of the study was to better understand the research process for these more intensive scholars, as well as to form a strong working relationship between the library and this department.

A task force was formed as a partnership between KU Libraries, the College of Liberal Arts and Sciences, and the Hall Center for Humanities (a research center). Through an 18-month series of meetings, focus groups, survey, and site visits we assessed readiness to develop a more formalized support system for digital humanities research.

Appreciative Inquiry (AI) is an established organizational development theory based on the belief that organizations change in the way they inquire (Cooperrider & Srivastava, 1987). In other words, you become what you study. As such, appreciating what is exemplary in an organization will lean an organization to discover how to create more excellence. The Business Library undertook this process starting with the engagement of two consultants who conducted focus groups with participants, including faculty members, students, and staff. Through stories and exploring themes, participants shared what was most successful about the library and how they envisioned this success could be extended into the future. These focus groups not only provided useful data, but were also a great way to publicly discuss the successes of the library and to engage stakeholders in positive conversation.

Brief survey distributed annually about specialized library services provided by one of our libraries.

Card sort analysis of library research and subject guides. RIOT- Information Literacy Tutorial.

Comparative, task-based usability study of current library website and revision prototypes.

Customer Satisfaction Survey continuously available on our website.

Facilities: observational studies were conducted to see how students currently use spaces. Results of study were combined with service-related metrics to determine what new furniture to purchase.

Faculty Journal Study: This was an in-depth analysis of LibQUAL+® data from across years and ARL institutions, to better understand faculty perceptions of journal collections. Individual phone interviews were also conducted with faculty on campus to gather more information about journal use and satisfaction with collections.

Graduate student focus groups.

"How do you love us?" Valentine's Day Raffle.

In 2002 and 2006, the UIC University Library participated in the LibQUAL+® Total Service Quality survey. In addition to providing comparable assessment information from peer institutions, the LibQUAL+® surveys compiled UIC library patron feedback on service quality. The surveys highlighted a need for greater access to technology and overall improvements to library facilities.

In progress. Study of graduate student needs to assist in creation of a general graduate study area as well as services targeted specifically at PhD students.

In the fall of 2009, we conducted usability tests of our new homepage and two newly redesigned websites, one about scholarly publishing and the other a new site for the Rotch Library of Architecture & Planning.

In the spring of 2009, the Penn Libraries began a new strategic planning effort. As part of an extensive environmental scan and information-gathering phase, we hired a consultant to facilitate a series of focus groups with university faculty and graduate students across disciplines. These focus groups were designed to examine their conceptions of "the library"; to explore their work habits and teaching, research, and study behaviors; and probe their attitudes towards training in information and technology proficiency.

LibQUAL+® survey will be administered this semester.

LibQUAL+® survey.

Re-architecting of Libraries web presence.

Redesigned the entry floor of the undergraduate library to encourage usage of student's own laptops as we planned to remove most of the library's public computers.

Setting up of a Library Student Advisory Group (LSAG) in 2009.

Student competition to redesign the main floor of the library and to make suggestions about the layout and use of services on other floors as well.

Student Information Seeking Behaviors study including faculty interviews and website evaluation.

Survey of all instruction activity conducted throughout organization.

Survey happens every two years. In 2009, the survey was done March 30 through April 5th. The survey was distributed to patrons entering the building at selected hours each day during the week.

The Dean of Libraries and selected team leaders regularly meet with the officers and library advisory boards Associated Students of the University of Arizona (primarily undergraduate) and the Graduate and Professional Students Council. They are provided with information about LibQUAL+® results and other student needs assessment activities that have identified areas of high importance or dissatisfaction along with some possible changes in or additions to the library's services. The students give feedback, identify additional services or resources that they think are needed, and together the group identifies priorities for use of the income from student fee and priorities for implementation if the fee is increased.

The Info Commons @ Langsam Survey is an annual survey conducted since 2002 during a one-week period in spring quarter. The purpose of the survey is to get more information about our users, how they use our libraries and our resources, and their satisfaction with our service.

The Libraries sought to increase the accessibility and findability of its collection through the use of a new discovery interface tool.

The library engaged in many assessments around the creation of a new catalog interface.

The library website user needs project aims to collect information on the current usability of our website navigation, terminology, and content in order to improve it. It also aims to collect information on user needs, user preferences, and user terminology to plan for new user requirements, new information architecture, and new navigation.

To create an entry point to library resources for every course on campus, to tailor the content of each course as much as possible, and to provide a scalable and sustainable system to deliver this content to students.

University Archives and Rare Books & Special Collections Survey. The survey examined user satisfaction in these two branches with four services: facilities, staff services, website, and finding aids, in addition to gathering information on general usage and user demographics. Anyone who had used the services in the past was invited to complete the survey.

Usability studies of the library's website.

Usability testing.

Usability testing of library website to facilitate redesign. Tested several times over the course of the project.

Usability testing of new website.

We are currently assessing library branch usage and needs for a particular clientele group.

We are renovating a large space in O'Neill Library and also in the process are rethinking how and what service should happen at a single service point. Eventually, I think this desk will be seen as a starting point for all campus services.

We asked the student advisory board to divide into small groups and use Flip cameras to identify areas around the library that needed improvement. The groups were assigned various floors and asked to both film and narrate what improvements needed to be made.

We conducted a poll on our library's main web page to determine what mobile devices people use for accessing the library's website.

We conducted a website usability study.

We have conducted several usability studies of the library's catalog, web pages, and physical spaces.

We observe students and faculty using our website to conduct several common tasks.

We performed 15 (1/2 hour) card-sorting sessions with a mix of graduate students and undergrads to inform the language used on the primary tabs of our library home page, and the structure of those tabs. Participants rearranged, ranked, and renamed the tabs to help us to understand what makes the most sense to them.

We recently finished a semester long project to conduct a series of evaluations on our library catalog. Each phase had a different goal: have an open discussion with library staff to discuss what is working and what isn't; to do an overall assessment (heuristic evaluation) to find problem areas; to gauge satisfaction with searching overall vs. known item searches vs. subject searches; to fine-tune labels used to describe items that have full text available; to test proposed functionality changes.

We recently held a week-long thesis camp for senior honors students in collaboration with the Writing Center and the Center for Undergraduate Scholarly Engagement. The program fit in very well with one of the major goals of the College of Arts & Letters to "increase the intensity and sophistication of our undergraduate education" and is a good example of reaching out to users based on their activities and needs.

We used a short in-person survey with students to gather feedback on tabletop signage that promoted our reference services.

We worked with a class to redesign and renovate a branch library in the business school. The class used the library as a case study and we implemented selected recommendations from all of the case studies submitted.

Website redesign.

Website redesign and development of LibGuides.

Whole redesign of new service. Bringing together Data Resources Library, Serge A. Sauer Map Library, and Government Publications service into one service.

20. **Is the target of the activity any typical library user or a specific category of user (e.g., faculty, graduate students, etc.)? N=51**

Any user	23	45%
A specific category of user	28	55%

If you answered "A specific category of user," please identify the category.

Faculty and graduate student users.

Faculty and graduate students in the cultural anthropology department.

Faculty and graduate students in the humanities.

Faculty, graduate students, and staff in particular departments.

Four types of users: graduates, undergraduates, librarians, and faculty.

Graduate students.

Graduate, undergraduate, faculty.

Pediatric residents.

PhD students and more generally grad students.

Primarily students.

Primarily undergraduates.

Senior honors students.

Students.

Students.

Students enrolled in courses and faculty.

Students using the library's group tables in the learning commons.

Students were the primary focus.

Those involved with the school of business.

Undergraduate and graduate students.

Undergraduate and graduate/professional students.

Undergraduate students.

Undergraduate students (with small number of graduate students also taking part).

Undergraduates.

Undergraduates.

Undergraduates and graduate students.

We choose participants representing faculty, undergraduates, graduate students, distance education, and foreign exchange students.

We targeted undergraduates, graduates, and faculty in equal measure.

21. **What is the source of funding for this activity? Check all that apply. N=50**

Library operating budget	46	92%
Special one-time funds	5	10%
Grant	1	2%
Other	6	12%

Please describe other source of funding.

Co-op funding for Co-op student (SLAIS graduate student).

Funds from College and Hall Center.

Library IT money.

No special funding was necessary.

There were also contributions from other support units and academic departments.

We used Survey Monkey and contributed staff time to design, implement, and compile the data.

ASSESSING THE USER EXPERIENCE

22. What tool(s) did/will your library use to evaluate or inform the user experience? Check all that apply. N=51

Surveys	27	53%
Focus groups	24	47%
Usability testing	21	41%
Anecdotal comments	16	31%
Suggestion box (physical or online)	9	18%
E-mail	5	10%
Design charrettes	4	8%
Social media	4	8%
Furniture trials	3	6%
Audio diaries	2	4%
Instruction session evaluations	2	4%
Video diaries	1	2%
Online discussion forums/message boards	1	2%
Other tool(s)	15	29%

Please specify other tool(s).

Analysis of existing data. Phone interviews.

Individual card-sorting sessions.

Interviews with participants were recorded and transcribed for analysis and use in writing the final report.

Interviews—both student and faculty—photo diary, mapping exercise, web page redesign activity.

Log file analysis.

Site visits to other institutions.

Some students contacted the library re. class assignments where they had to assess a process on campus. Some students chose to work on library space planning and reported their findings to the library administration.

The library-wide LibQUAL+® survey did not suffice as an indicator of service quality for the smaller, specialized collections, such as University Archives and Rare Books and Special Collections. This new survey reached the intended audience more effectively.

Usage data.

Use statics for electronic resources and the online catalog (The CAT).

Use stats analysis of log files & using Google Analytics. Informal "budget" usability testing methods. Heuristic evaluation. Staff feedback discussion.

We also interviewed participants after they had completed the usability study.

We have ongoing involvement of students in assessment of the website through a class assignment from an Information and Computer Sciences professor.

We worked with a class to redesign and renovate a branch library in the business school. The class used the library as a case study and we implemented selected recommendations from all of the case studies submitted.

23. **Did/will your library send a direct invitation to potential participants or have an open recruitment of library users to participate in this activity or use both methods to recruit participants? N=51**

Open recruitment	16	31%
Direct invitation	14	28%
Both	21	41%

24. **What tools or outlets did/will your library use to recruit library users to participate in this activity? Check all that apply. N=51**

E-mail	32	63%
Library web page	29	57%
User contact from subject specialist/faculty liaisons/bibliographers	22	43%
Posters and/or flyers	18	35%
In-house media (library newsletters, for example)	17	33%
Giveaways (bookmarks, pens, pencils, etc.)	12	24%
Social media	12	24%
Cover letter attached to survey	6	12%

Campus media (newspaper, radio, TV)	5	10%
Local media (newspapers, radio, TV)	1	2%
Other	20	39%

Please specify other tools or outlets.

Agenda item at student advisory board meeting.

Class assignments for an Information & Computer Sciences class.

Contact with student groups on campus.

Department chair recruited candidates at faculty meeting.

Direct contact with relevant constituents.

Discussion with leaders in stakeholder areas to identify key participants.

Electronic signage.

E-mail addresses retrieved from circulation records.

For one study, we approached students as they entered the library, offering Hershey bars in exchange for their time filling in a quick survey about what they did while in the library that day.

Graduate Student Organization helped with initial recruitment.

In-person recruiting in high traffic areas.

On home page and 12 other library web pages.

Project website as well as library home page.

Students recruiting participants.

Students within a specific course.

Table set up in lobby to recruit volunteers.

The Dean of Libraries consulted with other deans and student offices for assistance in identify potential participants.

We call this a "guerilla" survey, where staff rove throughout the learning commons areas and ask students to engage with them about a topic, in this case a small placard promoting our services.

Word of mouth.

Worked closely with campus colleagues who run learning management systems and train faculty in their use (helped market to faculty).

25. Did/will your library offer any type of incentive to encourage users to participate in the activity? N=51

Yes	34	67%
No	17	33%

If yes, please indicate the type of incentive. Check all that apply. N=34

Food, drink, and/or candy	19	56%
Gift cards	17	50%
Cash payment	3	10%
Other prize or incentive	4	13%

Please specify other prize or incentive.

Each test taken allowed users an additional entry for a chance to win an iPad or an iTouch.

Food service for 1/2-hour sessions.

iPod Touch 8GB (quantity 5).

Lunch is provided at the advisory board meetings.

SHARING THE ASSESSMENT RESULTS

26. Did/will the library share the results of the assessment with others (funding/governing boards, users, etc.)? N=50

Yes	45	90%
No	5	10%

If yes, please briefly describe to whom the results are communicated, the method(s) used, and whether the communication method varies by audience. N=43

A brief overview of the results was presented at the 2010 Special Libraries Association Conference and a paper published in that conference's proceedings. Presented methodology and findings to Libraries and Cultural Resources Senior Leadership Team.

A final report was written summarizing the results of the interviews. The report was shared widely within the library and with the Cultural Anthropology department. Presentations have also been made at a local conference, the ARL assessment conference, and a poster was presented at another national conference.

All library staff, but primarily to Public Services Steering Committee, Virtual Access Committee, Web Program Director, Library Planning Council, and the Administrative Committee. Results were also shared with Library Board and Library Student Resource Group.

Brief results will be shared through the project website.

Following any big project we hold an open presentation for staff to discuss findings. We also put our final reports on our website. For this particular project, the group that conducted the work reports to a high level committee so results are also shared with that group.

Information has been shared broadly throughout the university and with governing board.

Internally and only with other librarians at a conference and in a published paper.

Libraries website - news feed e-mail to Faculty of Social Science primary users, Western Libraries staff, and university administration. Attended Department of Geography Faculty Council for presentation to answer questions.

Library administrators, Collections Associate University Librarian, Library Advisory Board, Library/Archives staff.

Plans are underway to share the information via our website and Facebook site.

Presentations at conferences (Virginia Library Association, Library Assessment Conference) and library staff meetings. Reports to library administration. Report to Information Technology and Communication division. Report to students who participated in project. Article in student daily newspaper.

Presentations to staff will be the major method.

Presentations will be made to Provost and Deans, faculty senate, student government groups, and departmental faculty.

Provost.

Public posted results on web, held several forums.

Reports available internally via Sakai site; presentations to internal and advisory groups; included in annual reports, reports on improvements, and other administrative reports; news items.

Results are communicated to staff through public meetings and the staff intranet. Results are analyzed within each broad department area.

Results have gone to administration. Thereafter, they will be e-mailed to our web office and others for whom they may be of interest. They will likely also be discussed by our library-wide group of web editors who will be charged with considering, and possibly making, the appropriate changes.

Results of the survey were shared with the designer of the sign and our communications director.

Results were communicated to focus group participants, to a graduate and professional student organization on campus, and to all standing faculty via a Penn Libraries newsletter edition devoted entirely to the strategic plan and planning process.

Results were presented at a conference. They were also shared verbally at the library's monthly management meeting and with the Chair of the Pediatrics Department.

Results were presented to library staff, Management Committee, the Collections and Services Directors, etc. Results were presented at the Library Assessment Conference 2010. Results will be shared with faculty once an action plan has been developed.

Results were shared with the library staff and the University Committee on Libraries.

Results will be communicated back to the departments and up to the Provost. There will likely be a campus newspaper article on the results.

Results will be communicated through professional presentation and/or publication, as well as through presentation to campus student advisory group.

Results will be shared with the university administration.

Select comments shared with advisory boards.

Students involved in the website assessment through their class assignment produce a report of the results, which is shared with future classes.

Study is not fully analyzed yet, but the Library Administrative Council will receive both a written and oral report. A briefer report will be presented in the library's Town Meeting. The study will be posted on the library intranet for any library employee to examine.

The Graduate School will receive a report on what we find are the biggest needs for PhD students.

The library website is being redesigned by The Office of Information Services & Technology and Creative Services. The library has communicated the results of the focus groups and usability testing to these groups.

The Penn State community through our Newswire, social media, Libraries' internal newsletter *Interview*.

The report was widely distributed to the campus through various media outlets following presentation to the Deans of the Libraries and College, Director of the Hall Center, and the Provost.

The resulting information is shared with the university administration (president and provost), the Library Cabinet (administrative group), and with specific teams affected and with all library staff. Memos (e-mail), written reports, and in-person communication are used with the university administration. In-person reports from the Dean are made to Library Cabinet and team leaders of targeted teams. E-mail and reports at all staff meetings are used to inform all library staff.

The results were published on an open website, as is our practice for all usability tests. We also sometimes speak at conferences and publish papers about our results.

The results were shared with the library facility manager.

The results will be shared in a journal of library and information science.

Varied by audience: direct contact, articles in library publications (internal and external), and presentations at conferences.

We have reported on LSAG activities on a semi-annual basis at the Library Council, and in the online faculty newsletter. We have reported on LSAG in the Libraries' Annual Report.

We shared this data with the Dean and University Librarian, our library staff, and the Provost. The data helps us to better understand our users, their needs, and to inform changes to our services and facilities. Communication methods varied and were targeted to the audience. Summary documents were shared. At times only specific data was shared with an individual that was relevant to the topic at hand.

We will share the results when the competition is completed.

DESIGN CHANGES

27. Please briefly describe any design changes that have been/will be made based on this user experience activity. N=47

A mobile site was designed to work on the devices that we discovered were used most frequently from doing the poll.

Adjustments were made to the Business Library's physical space, including replacing tables with modular furniture that could accommodate a variety of group sizes. Developed an improved delineation between quiet and collaborative spaces. Adjusted the Business Library website to make it more interactive, incorporate social media, and to increase awareness of services offered.

An area that had been planned for staff offices was reclaimed for student study with public services and technology staff on the perimeter of the study space. Group study rooms were added.

An Institute for Digital Research in the Humanities has been established with seed funding for two years. The home for the institute is within the KU Libraries' Center for Digital Scholarship. The co-directors are a librarian and a faculty member from the humanities.

Better way finding. Cleaner restrooms. Customer service training. Best Practices for Services.

Changed the signage, improved access procedures, reduced noise, reviewed policies (e.g., copying), followed up with further analysis of user groups.

Changes have been made in training our Peer Mentors to best meet the needs of the undergraduates. Understanding user needs has helped inform the work of the librarians. Changes have been made to the library website and to what is emphasized in library instruction classes. The survey results have also informed and supported facilities improvements such as varied study spaces (including support to create a 24/7 space in the library), spaces for laptops, and more electric to support laptops.

Complete redesign of library home page, investment in new integrative search tools (e.g., Ebsco's Discovery Services), changes to library catalogs, and new signage throughout buildings.

Complete redesign. So far have merged Data and Map resources and services to one location with the aim of better coordinated service delivery. Further implementation pending funding announcements.

Complete website redesign.

Continual improvement of library website and LibGuides to improve usefulness and usability.

Don't know yet.

Graffiti was removed in areas of the library that staff do not normally use (student study carrels).

Integration of the product into different learning technology systems in use on campus; adjustments in content, features, and design of the site. For the future: adding support for distance education classes, addressing specialized needs of science and technology majors, integrating faculty-suggested content customization, and providing more entry points into the system.

Library space layouts will change. Some spaces (e.g., collaborative study) will be enhanced with technology. More electrical outlets have been added to all the libraries.

Lots of minor changes. One thing that has come up before but we'll finally be addressing is that users are obviously searching the library catalog for individual articles (which it does not currently do). Short-term solution will be to add a message at top of search results, "Looking for articles? Try ArticlesPlus search!"

Major changes to structure.

More group study and quiet spaces, more wireless, more e-resources and e-services, better equipment (scanning/copying, computers/printers).

No changes as of yet because the competition is still in progress.

No changes have been made based on survey results.

None thus far, though once the results have been reviewed more widely, changes may be made to the design of our homepage and the language used there.

Over the past few years we have made iterative changes to the library's website based on the results of the focus groups and usability testing. The website is now being redesigned and the library has shared the user feedback with the designers.

Overhauled how facets are presented in the service (placement, number offered, field values) and we modified the search; other interface changes.

Redesign of website and supporting subject pages.

Renovation in O'Neil. Redesign of website (look and feel) adding content, working with campus instructional designers. Rethinking how bibliographers engage with departments, faculty, and students.

Renovation of one section of information commons area, with improved hardware and more robust suite of software/applications.

Results from these focus groups informed the major emphases of the Penn Libraries' strategic plan.

Several improvements were made to each of the three sites tested.

Signage will be redesigned to incorporate student feedback.

Significant changes to content, organization, and interactivity supported through library website.

Still compiling results, but will probably make changes in the website and in the physical landscape of the library buildings.

Subject guides results will be used to spark a library-wide discussion on design. RIOT will be revised based on faculty and student feedback.

The complete renovation of a branch library.

The experience has been eye opening, we have had good discussions with the group and they have given us useful feedback. They are contributing to development of our upcoming mobile-ready web pages; they helped with the development of library learning zones (quiet study, etc.); food policy changes, the design of the new catalogue interface. The LSAG has also participated in the planning, promotion, and hosting of the Learning Commons Opening.

The Libraries have recently completed a document that shifts the role of subject librarians from a collections focused model to engagement focused. This survey was seen as a model for how subject librarians might evaluate their departments to better understand the services the library can offer in order to partner in their research process. Several librarians have embarked on similar surveys of their assigned departments and have discovered new methodologies to uncover interesting findings.

The overall concept for the redesigned website was directly influenced by usability testing as were many, many smaller design decisions.

The project is the first phase of a full library website redesign. We expect it to impact our information architecture, navigation menus, preferred language, site features (e.g., gateways), and sub-site creation.

The study is not analyzed enough to determine findings and recommendations or to receive approval for implementation.

The website had a complete redesign to make it more accessible, up-to-date, and responsive to user needs. Continued review and formal usability testing to be held this spring will further improve the website.

There were major modifications to the layout of the floor. Many outlets were added, seating was replaced, new tables with different configurations were added, space was reallocated, and we acquired a fish tank.

These surveys served as a catalyst for deeper assessment activities and, ultimately, also contributed to the library's recent technology upgrades and facilities improvements.

We are looking at addressing three aspects of journal services in response to the data: outreach, interface design, collection development.

We are making immediate short-term simple fixes as well as developing in the long-term a completely new website based on our findings.

We have increased the number and variety of equipment that we provide for check out by library users. We have increased the number of group study rooms. We have added carrels that graduate students can "check out" for short-term use. We have added presentation practice rooms and equipment.

We received further justification for a graduate study room and a better understanding of the type of space and services that should be included. PhD focus groups will assist in the creation of services targeted at PhD students.

We redesigned the website and have since made minor modifications based on feedback.

We will decide which branch to close and ways to mitigate the closure on the most effected users.

27. **How would you characterize the impact of these changes on the user experience? N=44**

Major modification(s) to the existing design	17	39%
Minor modification(s) to the existing design	11	25%
Complete redesign	8	18%
Other	8	18%

Please describe other impact.

Depending on the issue, some major changes and some minor.

Development of a new product, with major modifications in the iterations as a result of users' suggestions.

New design.

Not sure at this time.

Partial: we weren't able to make all changes because the project is not finished.

Since this is an ongoing endeavor, we have used the information for a complete redesign, but currently, we are using the information for minor modifications.

The changes we make may seem minor, but they help to create a more user-friendly environment in the learning commons where student feedback is taken into account as we develop our communication strategies.

This was an entirely new design.

USER GROUPS AND ADVISORY BOARDS

28. Does your library consult with any user groups or advisory boards (such as the Student Government Association, campus academic departments, community organizations, a Student Advisory Board, Faculty Senate Committee on Libraries, or Community Advisory Group) to design, conduct, or analyze user experience assessment activities, or to recommend or implement design changes? N=69

Yes	56	81%
No	13	19%

If yes, please identify up to three groups that consult with the library on the user experience and briefly describe the composition of the group, the role it plays, and representative outcomes achieved through the library's engagement with the group.

Group 1 N=53

Name of group	Composition	Role(s)	Outcome(s)
Advisory Committee on Library Policy (ACLP)	Faculty, university and library administrators, current students	Meets occasionally to hear reports and updates about the library, and provides advice on policy questions under consideration.	ACLP advice has occasionally affected library programs, priorities, and budget issues.
Chapman Learning Commons Student Advisory Committee	Students, library staff. Students include student senators, reps from student societies, and students at large.	Provide feedback on programs, services, and spaces.	A valuable asset to the library in soliciting and receiving feedback to improve programs, services, spaces.

Name of group	Composition	Role(s)	Outcome(s)
College library committees	Includes the branch library head and faculty members in colleges	To advise the branch head of changes in curriculum, research, etc and desired changes in service.	Ongoing relationship with branch library, responsive library service.
Faculty Library Advisory Committee	Associate Vice Provost and faculty with Library Dean	Communicate faculty concerns and Dean's. Dean can discuss trends and issues relevant to university library.	Dean has a platform for speaking to faculty.
Faculty Senate Committee on Libraries	Faculty members elected to serve two-year appointments	Advise and support.	Regular meetings, gathering input and support.
Faculty Senate Library and Information Resources Committee	Faculty appointed to the committee by the Faculty Senate	Advise the library, provide feedback on planned activities, and communicate library activities to the Faculty Senate.	Advise the library and communicate endorsement of planned activities to the Faculty Senate.
Faculty Senate Library Committee	Faculty	Advises University Librarian.	
Faculty Senate Library Committee	Dean of Libraries, library representative, and faculty from across campus	Advisory	
Faculty Senate Library Committee	Faculty members and library administrators	Serve as a channel for regular communication between the faculty and library.	Keep faculty up to date on library issues and challenges; gain support from faculty for library initiatives; improve services based on faculty feedback.
First Year Advisory Board	10 first-year students with diverse demographics, dormitories, and intended majors	Offer ideas and opinions on projects or changes the library is considering. Suggest changes based on their experience.	Helping library to reframe first year orientation. Working with library on planning and presenting a movie on the quad. Participating in renovation planning for library most used by first year students. Added additional whiteboards based on their suggestions.
General Faculty Council Library and Cultural Resources Committee	Faculty, graduate student, and student representation named by the university's General Faculties Council	To advise Libraries and Cultural Resources on needs of academic users.	
Graduate and Professional Student Assembly	Penn graduate and professional students	To represent the concerns and advocate on the behalf of all graduate students at Penn.	Changes to new OPAC design, creation of strategic emphases and initiatives.

Name of group	Composition	Role(s)	Outcome(s)
Graduate and Professional Student Library Advisory Committee	Graduate and professional students	Advisory on library services and policies, including proposed changes.	Input, reaction, discussion, illumination.
Graduate and Professional Students Council	Five elected officers, elected representatives from all University of Arizona colleges, and two support staff	In relation to the library, GPSC advises us on the needs of graduate students and priorities for use of the student fee.	Support for increases in student library fee (which is bundled with the campus IT fee) and identification of priorities for its use.
Indiana University Bloomington Faculty Council Library Committee	Faculty	Advisory, advocate, evaluator	Ongoing
Institutional Review Board	Faculty from various disciplines across campus	To ensure human subjects are "treated with dignity, adequately protected from risk and harm, and voluntarily give informed consent to participate in research."	Approval to proceed with research projects.
Libraries Committee	Representatives of academic faculty and staff from diverse disciplines/areas	To provide suggestions for initiatives; to provide feedback for ongoing development.	Information is shared with various UX staff to implement or investigate further.
Library Advisory Board	Alumni, donors, members of the community	Advisory council to the Kelvin Smith Library	
Library Affairs Advisory Committee	Faculty, students, administrators	To advise the Dean.	
Library Policy Advisory Committee	Faculty members elected by the Faculty Senate	Advice on surveys, focus group, testers.	Faculty view and input on library matters. Improved services to faculty and graduate students.
Library Student Advisory Board	30–40 undergraduate students and 2–4 graduate students, OIT staff representative, Library Dean, head of Public Services, User Experience team, Circulation representative	To provide ideas and suggestions for both short-term and strategic changes to the library collections, facilities, operations, and services.	Ideas suggested by students on the advisory board often become reality over time. Furthermore, their input can be communicated directly to the library administration (head of Public Services and Library Dean) at Board meetings.
Library Student Advisory Committee	Students of all classifications	Advise the library on policies, procedures, and planning.	Ideas integrated into strategic planning as well as into our foundation work.

Name of group	Composition	Role(s)	Outcome(s)
Library Student Resource Group	Representative group of students from college, graduate programs, and professional schools	Advise library on user needs and communicate information about library to peers.	Provided input on survey, recommended changes to library renewal policies, etc.
Rutgers University Libraries Advisory Committee	Teaching faculty and administrators from student life, university press, and continuous education	"...to provide advice to the University Librarian to ensure that the programs, services, and collections of the University Libraries meet the research, instruction, and service priorities of the community."	Information sharing and advice.
Senate Committee on Libraries	Faculty and students	Advisory	Supported recommended changes.
Senate Library Committee	12 faculty and professional staff and 4 students	Advisory/consultative	Provide recommendations to the University Senate.
Student Advisory Board	Students, both undergraduate and graduate	Advisory on a variety of library services.	Improved services and user satisfaction.
Student Advisory Board	Open to any interested student	Provide input on programs and services.	Gives students a voice; they have provided valuable perspectives on priorities related to technology and facilities.
Student Advisory Board	Students from various colleges	Provides student input on services, resources, facilities.	Varies depending on input.
Student Advisory Board (undergraduate) - Relates to Activity 1	Approximately 9 students	Evaluation furniture, design	Affirmed that we are moving in the right direction.
Student Advisory Committee	Undergraduate and graduate students	Advisory	Hours changed; furniture changed; vending machines changed.
Student Advisory Group	Students and library staff	Student-driven library concerns are raised.	Hopefully, changes made.
Student Government		The Dean communicates with this group.	
Student Government Association (SGA)	Comprised of elected undergraduate representatives, SGA is the official representative group of all undergraduate students attending UC.	Partnered with the Libraries and UC IT to secure funding for a 24/7 space in the library.	24/7 study/computer space created in the library along with a quiet study area.

Name of group	Composition	Role(s)	Outcome(s)
Student Library Advisory Board (SLAB)	Ten or more graduate and undergraduate students that broadly represent the academic programs and overall diversity of the UNC student body	Provide feedback and advice on library services and resources in support of both grad and undergrad student study and research needs.	
Student Library Committee	Student representatives from the three major campus student government organizations	Advisory and advocacy	Advise on services and collections.
Student Representative Roundtable	Vice-President Students and Student Representative of the York University Board of Governors co-chair, and they appoint the membership which consists of the Chair of Senate, students, student support providers and reps from student government.	The SRR provides advice, guidance, and information that will assist in the development of policies, procedures, and action plans that promote the engagement of students in the academic and social life of York.	They have provided feedback on 24-hour library service; we have raised awareness of our services and obtained a great volunteer for our LSAG.
Survey Research Centre	See: http://www.src. uwaterloo.ca/	Help design surveys and provide advice on activities such as usability protocol.	Better designed surveys, etc.
The Howard Undergraduate Student Association (HUSA)	Undergraduate students—all levels and disciplines	Comment on library facilities, resources, equipment, and services and suggest changes to the same.	Implementation of several suggestions and the highest consideration of all others.
Undergraduate Student Government	UIC undergraduate students	Represents undergraduate students' interests.	Longer library hours; more computers; improved computer software; Learning Commons planning.
University Committee on Libraries	Elected faculty from the various colleges; graduate student representative; undergraduate student representative	The University Committee on Libraries reviews policies and practices relating to library resources and services and provides oversight of the development of the libraries. The UCL serves as one of the primary interfaces and communications links between the Libraries and other campus units responsible for providing information resources and services and the university community at-large.	

Name of group	Composition	Role(s)	Outcome(s)
University Council on Research Activities and Libraries	Faculty, Deans, Administrators, including the University Librarian	Advise the President and Provost.	Better communication among key groups on campus.
University Librarian's Student Advisory Committee	Undergraduate and graduate students from all academic colleges	Advisory to University Librarian; communication with broader student body.	
University Library Committee	University faculty and librarians	Advisory to Dean of Libraries	
University Library Committee	Representative with strong representation of faculty	Provide advice to the Dean of Libraries.	Input into decision-making process.
University Library Committee	7–10 faculty appointed by the University Senate for two-year terms	Review strategic directions, endorse major policy changes, discuss new services, and provide general advice to the Dean of Libraries.	Library gains an important perspective from faculty who represent different disciplines. Committee members are able to explain library issues to their colleagues.
University Library Committee	Dean of Libraries (as Secretary), 9 elected faculty representatives from various colleges (one as Chair), graduate student representative, undergraduate student representative, Director of Financial Affairs (Student Services)	The University Library Committee (ULC) reviews, consults, and advises on, plans for, and receives reports and recommendations on the performance of library services, automation, budget, administrative structure, and allocation of resources. Responsibility for keeping the faculty informed of major issues and for creating opportunities for the faculty to discuss priorities also falls to the committee.	
University Senate Library Committee	Faculty, library staff, graduate students, undergraduate students	Advisory	

Name of group	Composition	Role(s)	Outcome(s)
University Senate Library Committee	Committee is composed of a committee chair from the University faculty, 5–6 faculty members and the Dean of Libraries.	The committee is charged with the responsibility for recommending to the University Senate policies to promote the educational interests of the university as a whole with respect to the Libraries. The SLC is responsible for consultation and advising with faculty of the Libraries or the Dean of Libraries, on such matters as are referred to it by the by the Libraries faculty, by the Dean, or by other university personnel, which pertain to improving the effectiveness of the Libraries as a part of the broad academic program of the University of Kentucky.	In the past, the committee has worked with the Libraries in sponsoring and promoting effectiveness efforts and other issues of importance to the research and educational programs.
University Student Advisory Council	Student representatives from each college on campus	Contribute to the central role of the academic experience in the life of the student; consult and advise.	Impetus for Library Use study.
University Students' Council	Executive	Advisory, stakeholders and advocates of appropriate behaviours.	Offering 24/7 library for study during April and December 2010.
UO Student Federation	Student	Representation of students	We introduced group room, calm floor instead of quiet floor, etc.
Vanderbilt Student Government	President and representatives	Advise on needs for library renovation.	More group studies and café and increased power outlets integrated into final plan; students voted special recognition for library and staff by student government.

Name of group	Composition	Role(s)	Outcome(s)
Administrative Board of the Library	Fourteen members, including faculty, librarians, and graduate/undergraduate students	An advisory board to the University Librarian	
Associated Students of the University of Arizona	Three elected officers and ten elected at-large student representatives	In relation to the library, ASUA advises us on the needs of primarily undergraduate students and priorities for use of the student fee.	Support for increases in student library fee (which is bundled with the campus IT fee) and identification of priorities for its use.
Faculty Academic Senate Committee	Faculty from various disciplines	Advisory	Note: The formation of this committee is underway.
Faculty Senate Committee on University Libraries	Faculty, graduate, and undergraduate student representatives, campus library directors	Advise the library on policies and procedures relating to operations, facilities, and budget of the libraries.	
Friends of Morris Library Board	Alumni and Community	To support the library.	
Friends of the Libraries Executive Committee and Sub-committees	Member of the Libraries Friends	Advisory/consultative	Targeted fundraising for specific collections.
Graduate Student Council	UIC graduate students	Represents graduate students' interests.	Selection of electronic resources; addition of specialized research instruction workshops.
Graduate Student Council	President and representatives	Advise on needs for library renovation.	Changes in cafe hours to favor longer evening hours.
Graduate Students Association (GSA)	All graduate and professional students at Howard	Suggest new resources, equipment, and facilities.	Implementation of several suggestions and the highest consideration of all others.
GWUL Development Advisory Board	Donors, some alumni, some faculty, and library administrators	Advisory to the library administration on fund raising activities.	Identification of new prospects, increased donations to the library.
Learning Studio Assessment Committee	Representatives from the Libraries, Student Success, and IT	Advising, planning	Conducting regular assessment efforts to determine new directions for the Learning Studio.
Library Advancement Council	10–12 current or prospective library donors appointed by the Dean	Fundraising, building external support for the library, providing external perspective for the Dean.	Increased financial support for the library, good alumni relationships.
Library Advisory Council	Faculty, administration, students	Advisory	

Name of group	Composition	Role(s)	Outcome(s)
Library Board	Representative group of faculty	Advise library on faculty needs and communicate information about library to other faculty members.	Approved changes to policies (e.g., privacy, fees), advised on budget reduction, and supported participation in Google digitization initiative.
Library Faculty Advisory Board	20–25 faculty representing every college. Representatives from the library include the User Engagement Librarian, the Library Dean, the Associate Deans, the head of the Faculty Engagement Department, and the head of the Scholarly Publishing and Digital Services Department.	The faculty advisory board focuses primarily on the collection (especially the journal collection) and services that faculty tend to utilize most frequently, such as ILL and document delivery processes. The board serves as an advocate on behalf of the library to the Provost and other institute administrators.	Due in part to the faculty advisory board's efforts, the library received special one-time funding from the Provost to purchase a large collection of critical science and technology journals.
Library Student Advisory Committee	Student representatives from the various schools	To provide suggestions for initiatives; to provide feedback for ongoing development.	Information is shared with various UX staff to implement or investigate further.
Library Student Advisory Council	Student library employees	Study library facilities, processes and services and make proposals to the library administration.	Study area in library with piped-in music and other projects.
MBA Marketing Team Composition - Relates to Activity 1	6 teams	Assessed undergrad experience in Libraries; interviewed approximately 1,000 students.	Told us we needed to change our spaces; key driver in change.
Medical Student Association	8 students (2 from each class)	To advise the College of Medicine Dean, Sr. Associate Dean, Health Sciences Library (HSL) Director on student-related matters.	24/7 computer lab space was created for medical students as a result of this group seeing the need and working with the College of Medicine administration and the HSL Director to implement.
Office of Research Ethics	See: http://iris.uwaterloo.ca/ethics/	Ensure that assessment projects comply with ethics standards.	Ethics approval.
One-on-one meetings on ad hoc basis	Dean/Associate Deans of colleges/student groups	To determine how the library can better serve college needs.	Advice and direction.
Planning and Institutional Research, University Administration	Senior Planning analysts	Advising assessment librarian on protocols, policies, methodology; partner in conducting LibQUAL+® and other surveys.	Preparation and implementation of effective survey methodologies and strategies.

Name of group	Composition	Role(s)	Outcome(s)
Rutgers University Student Assembly	Student leaders	Student government body that represents the undergraduate student population of Rutgers-New Brunswick.	Information sharing and advice.
Student Government Association Library Committee	SGA representatives appointed to the committee	Advisory	Provide general feedback; request new services and enhancements; sounding board for planned initiatives.
Student Government (various committees)	Elected students	Make recommendations to library to support prioritized initiatives.	
Student Government Association	Elected students	Provides student feedback to University Librarian.	
Student Government Association	Students	On an occasional basis, the Libraries have worked with and consulted student government about issues related to library service.	Services and policies relating to students have been addressed. (e.g., extension of hours, food and beverages in the library).
Student Government Association	Elected undergraduate students	Communicate student concerns to be addressed by Dean.	Dean has a platform for speaking to student representatives.
Student Government Association	Elected student representatives	Provide student input on library space, activities, policies, and procedures.	Higher student engagement in library activities.
Student Library Advisory Board	Undergraduate and graduate students	Serve as a channel for regular communication between the student representatives and library administration.	Better understand how the library can serve students at all levels.
Student Library Advisory Committee	Undergraduate students	Advisory on library services and policies that affect undergraduates	Input, reaction, discussion, context
Undergraduate Advisory Board	10 sophomores through seniors with diverse demographics, living arrangements, and majors	Offer ideas and opinions on projects or changes the library is considering. Suggest changes based on their experience.	Lengthened the hours of the library cafe. Creating inspirational quotes for the stairwells. Increased the number of healthy snacks in the vending machines.
Undergraduate Student Libraries Advisory Council	Elected representative undergraduate students in various majors	Meets periodically with the Dean of Libraries to discuss matters involving undergraduates and the Libraries experience.	

Name of group	Composition	Role(s)	Outcome(s)
Undergraduate Student Library Advisory Group	Voluntary undergraduate students	Sounding Board, Advisory	Ongoing
University Council Committee on Academic and Related Affairs	University faculty, staff, and students	To advise the vice provost and director of libraries on the policies, development, and operation of the university libraries.	
University Libraries Committee	Faculty and a representative from student government	Provides faculty input on services, resources, facilities.	Varies depending on input.
University Library Committee	Faculty and student representatives (appointed)	Advise on policies, services, space.	Perceived as an active committee that makes a difference; members raise concerns and are committed to their role.
University Library Committee	Faculty representatives appointed by Faculty Senate	Advisory and advocacy	Advise on services and collections.
UO Graduate Student Federation	Graduate Students	Representation of graduate students.	We dedicated a full floor to their needs (study carrel with key, nice quiet study room, mentor service, etc.)
Various student associations on campus	Student government representatives	Advising, outreach, assessment support, general sounding-board for gathering ideas and hearing issues.	Mixed, some student associations are more active than others.
York Federation of Students	Undergraduate student union	Advocacy	Collaboration with student union executive on certain initiatives.

Group 3 N=24

Name of group	Composition	Role(s)	Outcome(s)
Bamboo Shoots	Library administration, library and university IT support, humanities faculty	Identify ways to improve library support for faculty who want to build collections of digital objects for their research and teaching.	
Dean's Student Advisory Committee	15–18 juniors and seniors who have been selected as residential advisors for first year students	Bring student issues to the Dean's attention; serve as student advisors on specific library projects.	Better and more responsive services for students, particularly undergraduates.

Name of group	Composition	Role(s)	Outcome(s)
Faculty [Senate] Council on University Libraries	Elected faculty members (voting), representatives from student and staff groups (ex-officio)	Policy issues related to collection development; services; space needs; and budgetary requirements.	Input, support, and advocacy.
Faculty Liaisons	At least one faculty representative from each degree-granting academic department	Inform librarians about departments' needs and participate in the development/review of library collections.	Recommendations drive decisions regarding new purchases, journal cancellations, and service innovations.
Faculty Senate Committee on Libraries	Faculty elected or appointed, university administration, university librarian	Advocacy for the library, to keep faculty informed of developments in library services, budgets, etc.	Improved relations between the library and the faculty, support for additional funds and/or to halt reductions.
Focus Groups of faculty and students	Selected based on assessment topic	Advisory	Opening the Libraries Info Commons, coffee shops, and Undergraduate Virtual Library.
Georgia Tech Student Media	Student Radio Station; Literary Arts Magazine; Student Newspaper; Student Research Journal	The library collaborates with WREK on a weekly library radio show ("Lost in the Stacks"). In addition, the library supports the undergraduate research journal ("The Tower"), and also partners with "Erato" the student literary/arts journal. Through formal and informal contacts, library staff often receive feedback from these students regarding library facilities, services and resources.	The library radio show has allowed the library to simultaneously market the program to a wider student and non-student audience. The partnerships with the undergraduate research journal and the student literary/arts journal have positioned the library as being strong supporters of both the science/technology focus of the Institute, as well as the arts and humanities at Georgia Tech.
Graduate and Professional Student Council	Representatives of the graduate and professional school student body	Offer ideas and opinions on projects or changes the library is considering. Suggest changes based on their experience.	Library creating Responsible Conduct of Research Forums, which all graduate and professional school students must attend as part of graduation requirement. Investigating possibility of dedicated graduate student space in library.
Graduate and Professional Student Organization	Graduate Students	Sounding board, advisory, partner	Ongoing

Name of group	Composition	Role(s)	Outcome(s)
Graduate School and SGA Town Hall Meeting	Graduate school faculty and students	Communicate student concerns to be addressed by the Dean.	Problems are identified and followed up by the Dean.
Graduate Student Association Library Advisory Board	Appointed members of the GSA	Advisory	Provide general feedback; request new services and enhancements; sounding board for planned initiatives.
Graduate Student Libraries Advisory Council	Elected representative graduate students in various fields	Meets periodically with the Dean of Libraries to discuss matters involving graduate students' experiences in the Libraries.	
Health Professions Student Council	Students from the Medical College	Represents medical students' interests.	Longer hours; new seating; safer parking options; additional security in evenings.
LibQUAL+® Steering Committee and LibQUAL+® Theme Teams	Librarians and library staff volunteer	Advise on survey management, marketing, publicity, implementation, analysis, and communications.	Effective survey implementation, outreach, shared knowledge, advocacy for improving services.
Libraries and Academic Resources Committee, New Brunswick Faculty council	Combination of teaching and library faculty	Considers library priorities, collection growth, and needs.	Information sharing and advice.
Library Advisory Council	Business, community and campus leaders	Advisory and advocacy	Increased visibility with those communities and a greater success in fundraising.
Library and Scholarly Communications and Advisory Council	Representative from all colleges on campus	Advise library on issues, assess library programs, and services that affect students, recommend actions that could improve library collections and services.	Input caused library administration to reconsider policy of public access to our library auxiliary storage area.
Open Access Advisory Council	Administrators, research faculty, librarians, and library staff	Advise the Dean of Libraries and her designates on implementation of Open Access.	Ensuring the growth in dissemination of KU research through open access. Ensuring that the institutional repository meets the needs of faculty.
Student focus groups	Students recommended by VSG and GSC members	Advise on need for renovation, and library needs in general.	Studies to determine costs for longer hours for main library, agreements to continue these types of meetings.

Name of group	Composition	Role(s)	Outcome(s)
Undergraduate & Graduate Student Advisory Boards	Undergrad board consists of undergrads at University Park Campus; Grad board consists of graduate students at University Park Campus.	Undergraduates provided input on services offered.	Undergrad Advisory Board outcome: The Libraries adjusted service portfolio accordingly; Graduate Advisory Board outcome: Just beginning the process.
Undergraduate Student Government and Graduate Student Senate	Student government leadership	Source of feedback	Suggestions and changes from a student perspective.
University of Arizona Faculty Senate	Elected members from each UA college, 20 at large members, ex officio voting members including the President, the Provost, the Chair of the Faculty, the Vice Chair of the Faculty, the Secretary of the Faculty, the chair of the Strategic Planning and Budget Advisory Committee, the chair of the Undergraduate Council and the chair of the Graduate Council, one member representing the Vice Presidents and one member representing the Deans.	The Dean provides annual updates on the library and our services. The Dean also provides and seeks feedback, as needed, on issues such as spending reductions/serials cuts.	Better understanding among faculty of changes in services necessitated by budget cuts or lack of budget increases.
User Feedback and Assessment Committee	8 members and 2 co-chairs comprised of library staff from across the University Library system	Advance the library's goal of solidifying a service culture based on the assessment of library user needs and desires.	Develop staff training and resources to support assessment activities across the library system; track assessment and other research efforts underway in the library; advise library staff and library units who wish to conduct assessment projects; conduct small- and medium-scale assessment projects (e.g., targeted surveys, focus-groups, other methods); and implement, evaluate, analyze, and share findings of large-scale library-wide assessment projects (e.g., LibQUAL+®).

Name of group	Composition	Role(s)	Outcome(s)
Visiting Committee to the Library	Appointed by the Board of Trustees of the University	Serve as advisors and act as advocates for the library as well as act as liaisons to university administration.	Received advice and counsel on programs, collections, and operations, as well as financial support.

OTHER OUTREACH ACTIVITIES

30. Please briefly describe examples of new or innovative outreach measures your library has employed to seek input from existing or potential users relating to library services, resources, facilities, and/or technology. N=38

At present our methods are fairly standard surveys, suggestion box comments, and informal feedback from conversations with students in the library and student government feedback that varies with the interests of the SGA presidents. We also had a major space study done by which involved interaction with focus groups including a student group. This interaction carried a lot of weight with our Dean and brought about some changes as well as many of the ideas mentioned previously in this survey. We are exploring social media communications for further outreach.

At the time we created them, many of the methods used in the undergraduate research project were innovative, e.g., mapping and photo diaries. These methods have been adopted by dozens of libraries across the country.

Box on website asking for input, Facebook, Twitter.

College and Interdisciplinary Teams (CITs). Reorganized library staff that work with various campus departments and programs into teams. "Faster" initiative to shorten time from order to desktop. VITL (Visual, Information and Technology Literacy task force), campus group focusing on broad-based literacy programs.

Conducting faculty lunches through the Center for Teaching Excellence to gather input from faculty. Interacting with Student Senate for an organized input mechanism from student representatives.

Created a renovation LibGuide that includes a form for sending comments or questions.

Design charettes for planning an undergraduate space. Cafe naming contest. E-ssential – online newsletter for faculty. Facebook. Clickers in instruction to assess learning. LibGuides. Webinars sponsored by Continuous Education that featured librarians.

Direct feedback from users of our group study rooms, both first-come, first-served and reserveable rooms. The results of LibQUAL+® and analysis of questions, complaints, and feedback from customers identified access to and use of group studies to be of particular interest to students. We hope to better understand their experience and needs to inform potential changes or improvements in the way in which we provide access to these rooms.

During the fall of 2009, student workers in the library surveyed other students about their use of the library. If the respondents reported using the library, they were asked why they came to the library and what they did in the library. If the respondents reported not using the library, they were asked why not. The findings informed their development of an ongoing advertising campaign that includes posters, blog postings, and videos.

Each week, members of the library staff interview Georgia Tech students, faculty, and staff about their research and library-related issues on a radio show called "Lost in the Stacks." The User Engagement librarian periodically visits student organization meetings to solicit feedback from students about library facilities, resources, and services. Visits have also included ethnic student organizations (India Club, for example), as well as activities-based organizations (literary/arts journal, video gaming club). A proactive approach to engaging users via social media such as Twitter and Facebook. Specifically, the User Experience department follows student time-lines on Twitter and searches for mentions of the library or library-related discussion on Twitter.

Engage students in charrettes; engage students in the design of furniture, e.g., study carrels and chairs and based design on their feedback; work with System Design classes so that the students use the library as a "client" for some of their course work; inviting e-comments from students on various issues and posting them (anonymously) for the entire community to see; a series of "quick polls" on our home page intended to get feedback while also educating students about some of our services.

For all new initiatives announced on our website, we provide a link for users to "Send us feedback." Also, we have plans underway to begin hosting online forums via Facebook and Twitter later this spring. Via these forums, users will be able to offer us suggestions as well as share best practices related to their library experiences.

In addition to all the traditional methods we use (a/b testing, log analysis, usability, participatory design, ethnographic research methods, space design, etc.) we also like to mine social networking for reactions and to help us build use cases. Last fall we also had a UX photo booth at a new student orientation party where we asked students to pose for pictures with a sign they filled in "My ideal library _____." We are also trying to integrate a new tool for staff (and maybe the public in the future) to submit UI requests.

In planning the Libraries' new and forthcoming Knowledge Commons, a variety of measures were employed to gain user feedback relevant to new and existing library services. Students helped test and provide feedback on new technology for the Knowledge Commons, including collaborative computing solutions. Similarly, undergraduate students helped test furniture designs for the Commons, providing feedback on optimal workspace layout, types of chairs and tables, location of desktop computers, etc. Several architecture students conducted a study of an existing computer lab in the Libraries and their recommendations (utilization of "green walls," quick, stand-up computer access areas) were also integrated into the final plans for the new space.

Last year I began making visits, with the head of reference and the liaison librarian, to department chairs to have conversations about library services which have been a great way to gather information. We revamped our suggestion/comment mechanism by starting a suggestion blog where we now post all suggestions and responses - not innovative but new for us. During a project to gather feedback about our physical space we put poster boards on easels around the library and other locations on campus with different questions about the library. We are soon going to implement the Counting Opinions LibSAT which will be an ongoing satisfaction survey integrated into our website.

Marketing department advertises everything from individual instruction opportunities. They use banners and table tents and several video monitors throughout the library to advertise events, services, and resources. In the latest campaign, they are making short videos of the reference librarians called "meet your personal librarian." The library home page currently advertises the library mobile website.

One new outreach measure includes the introduction of online and physical suggestion boxes as a forum for patrons to express feedback, one-off problems, requests and/or compliments. The presence of the physical and virtual suggestion boxes communicates to patrons that their feedback is valued and strengthens the library's commitment to assessment and improvement. Additionally, beyond existing users, the library is also committed to reaching potential users. All of the surveys the library conducts go out to the entire university population (not just existing users) in an effort to better understand who does and does not use the library, and how the library can best serve the entire UIC community.

Online card sorting to help test terminology and groupings of subject areas on the website. Individual interviews with faculty regarding their research process (not directly asking about the website). Helpful in understanding which resources and services should be more prominent.

Online questionnaires have been tried over the years including the customer satisfaction survey.

Other than outreach and liaison services, we have not pursued situations where we are asking faculty/students to participate in these types of discussions.

Pizza with the Dean Late Night at the Library for incoming freshmen Stress-free Zone during finals week. Reception for International Students.

Simple web survey on the homepage of the library's website. Informal surveys on Facebook. Paper surveys at service points with raffle prize at completion. Student competitions to rethink or redesign something.

Strategic Planning Focus Groups; Furniture trials; Ongoing library instruction session assessments that assist university in evaluating and assessing the core curriculum.

The Irving K. Barber Learning Centre: advisory group (campus and community) advises on services offered by the IKBLC. IKBLC website and newsletters also ask for feedback. Asian Library and Xwi7xwa Library reach out to their distinct communities in unique ways.

The Library Dean and the Director for Library Instruction and Campus Partnerships meet with about 3,000 freshman parents during the summer and share information about the library and what it can do for their daughters/sons and solicit their perspectives and expectations. The Director for Instruction and Campus Partnerships meets with all 100 faculty involved with First Year Programs to share information about library resources and services and to get their input. She also meets with the 56 Freshmen Interest Group (peer) Advisors several times during their training sessions to discuss library resources, facilities, and services. The Director for Library Instruction and Campus Partnerships attends and serves as a judge for the International Projects Fair. In this capacity she interacts with 20 internationally oriented students about how they used the libraries' resources and what would have made things better for them. The library is presenting a poster session during an upcoming on-campus Undergraduate Research Symposium.

Two ethnographic studies of library use and student information seeking behaviors. Plasma screens with promotional audio and video. Library Student Advisory council survey. Track Google alerts and how we are portrayed on blogs, Twitter, etc. Comment books for all library exhibits. Feedback from large (500) student employees. Feedback on Facebook page.

Two other committees of interest are the Research Commons Advisory Committee and the Data Services Advisory Committee. Both have a mix of library staff, students, and faculty.

We aggregate data from our social media accounts, send it to the AUL for Public Services, and then distribute it to the appropriate group for action. For a project to redesign a room as a graduate student space, we interviewed grad students individually while walking around the room rather than doing a design charrette or focus group. To attract users to participate in a usability study, we put an ad in our rotating banner on the library home page. That was very effective.

We are currently conducting a study on PhD humanities students with Cornell. This is our first grant-funded, full-scale collaborative assessment project.

We are creating a new personal librarian program for outreach to first year students planned to launch in fall 2011. We're exploring technology to enable persistent feedback on library web pages via Disqus or similar tools.

We have an active Twitter account and social media campaign. We have gotten our Graduate Student Association to post short surveys to their website, which graduate students are more apt to answer. Additionally, there is an outreach table once a week in the student center that captures feedback from users.

We have interviewed library users to develop and refine a set of "personas" originally created by Johns Hopkins University; we use these personas as "stand-ins" for our users when making initial design decisions for physical and virtual spaces. We also allowed library users to evaluate and suggest changes to furniture being considered for our new Mansueto Library, which resulted in changes to design and lighting fixtures.

We monitor Twitter to follow comments about our library; it's quite effective in identifying immediate concerns from our users, primarily students.

We routinely solicit input via Facebook, Twitter, and our blog. We conduct programs to bring our rare materials to people in a non-library setting; librarians hold office hours in their departments. We conducted LibQUAL+®.

We use standard tools to reach potential users: surveys (including LibQUAL+®), interviews, focus group interviews, observation, object analysis (web logs, questions asked), etc.

We've conducted online surveys about the library using a laptop at the student center. We conduct mini "guerilla" surveys in which small feedback/comment cards are distributed throughout the library to students for quick responses on, for example, the laptop borrowing program. We regularly host a table at the student center to market the library and gather student feedback. In this context, we've conducted quick online surveys using a laptop computer at the student center.

Welcome Week activities: tables at all undergrad orientation sessions and at the library to answer both student and parent questions regarding library services. Also informs students and parents how they can provide support for the library: parents' committee, Student Advisory Board, Friends of the Library.

When we introduced iPads, students had an opportunity to "test drive" and blog about their impressions; this visibility generated much interest and discussion in the broader campus community.

ADDITIONAL COMMENTS

31. **Please enter any additional information that may assist the authors' understanding of your library's user experience activities. N=20**

Anticipate assigning more specific responsibilities for user experience to other position(s) in the near future.

Assessment is a substantial part of our current strategic plan. We have created a new position (Coordinator of Assessment and Training) and the Assessment Steering Committee to lead and give meaning to the library's assessment activities. The strategic vision statement focuses on improving user services and assessment is one way we intend to do this.

Biggest successes have been versions of usability testing. The libraries' web pages have consistently been based on user input.

Please understand we have just recently begun discussions around organized efforts at assessing user experiences, so our experience is quite limited.

Since we now have a new department for User Experience, we will be conducting more frequent ethnographic and observational studies, beginning in the spring of 2011.

The associate librarians and librarians who function as instructional librarians, consultants, bibliographers, and guides are directly involved in nurturing the library users and providing informative programs and useful services. The reference technician and student workers in Founders also promote engagement.

The UX Team grew out of a grass roots community and became a semi-formal structure with the creation of a five-member team to work on specific projects. The library is currently in the throes of a major reorganization, and though the UX Team has been recognized as valuable, we do not yet know where, or whether, it will end up in the final structure.

Yes, we are doing other kinds of assessment about our services so that we can improve them and the experience. But I would say we are embarking on a broader initiative to better understand what it means to design and implement a user experience as a holistic environment is which every touch point is important to the totality of the library experience. This is much different than holding a focus group about the library website. Those types of assessments are important to create incremental change within unique parts of the library operation, but I think we are going for something that will help us to redefine what the library is for our user community and the experience we want them to have when they use all the difference things that make up our library environment.

There are many ways that we engage our user base in continuous quality improvement. The Dean and University Librarian and our College and Departmental Libraries have advisory groups comprised of faculty and students. We try to employ a variety of methods to elicit feedback from our users and we also try not to over survey the same users.

We are a team-based, customer-focused organization that is designed around the needs of our customers. We regularly employ more than a dozen assessment tools including LibQUAL+®, usability studies, and action gap surveys to better understand the expectations and needs of our customers, to measure their satisfaction, and to identify areas in need of improvement. We develop and use performance measures and quality standards at the library level, the team level, and the personal level to support progress toward the library's and the university's goals.

We are in the process of hiring a user experience director to centralize and rationalize these activities.

We are still largely getting started in the UX area. A LibGuide for the UX office was recently created, and that will help showcase the activities of the office and solicit feedback from users. We brought in Nancy Foster in January, to teach ethnographic skills to staff, and Steven Bell is coming in April to teach his approach to designing better libraries.

We conduct ongoing research on major interfaces (track log file use and searches) and we conduct usability tests. This has become embedded in the organization. We also are looking to expand with a new program for a student panel that will help recruit testers and we hope help design some fun outreach activities.

We have installed a technology "sandbox," where students can experiment with a range of new technologies and provide feedback. This will inform future purchases and technology plans. Much of our current user experience activities are focused on space/service needs for a new facility that will open in 2013. In addition, two proposed Fellows projects (one for graduate students and one for undergraduates in the fields of engineering and textiles) will examine what students feel they need to know about the library.

We see user experience activities as the natural outgrowth of public services and see no reason to uproot them from their home in order to stand alone.

RESPONDING INSTITUTIONS

University of Arizona

Arizona State University

Boston University

Boston College

Brigham Young University

University of British Columbia

University of Calgary

University of California, Irvine

University of California, Santa Barbara

Case Western Reserve University

University of Chicago

University of Cincinnati

University of Colorado at Boulder

Columbia University

Duke University

University of Florida

George Washington University

University of Georgia

Georgia Institute of Technology

University of Guelph

Howard University

University of Illinois at Chicago

University of Illinois at Urbana-Champaign

Indiana University Bloomington

Johns Hopkins University

University of Kansas

Kent State University

University of Kentucky

Library of Congress

Louisiana State University

University of Louisville

McMaster University

University of Manitoba

Massachusetts Institute of Technology

University of Miami

University of Michigan

University of Minnesota

National Archives and Records Administration

University of New Mexico

University of North Carolina at Chapel Hill

North Carolina State University

Northwestern University

University of Notre Dame

Ohio University

University of Oklahoma

University of Oregon

University of Ottawa

University of Pennsylvania

Pennsylvania State University

Purdue University

Rice University

University of Rochester

Rutgers University

University of Saskatchewan

University of South Carolina

Southern Illinois University Carbondale

Syracuse University

Temple University

University of Texas at Austin

Texas Tech University

University of Utah

Vanderbilt University

University of Virginia

University of Washington

Washington State University

Washington University in St. Louis

University of Waterloo

University of Western Ontario

Yale University

York University

REPRESENTATIVE DOCUMENTS

User Experience Planning and Organization

SHARPENING OUR VISION

Duke University Libraries Strategic Plan (2010-2012)

1 Improve the User Experience

1.1 Frame a systematic process for collecting and sharing information about the ways library users work.

1.2 Use a better understanding of user communities to create extensive and deep collaboration with users at earlier stages of their research and teaching.

1.3 Institutionalize innovation by employing results from user assessments to improve procedures and services quickly.

1.4 Present library programs and services in ways that help users understand the connections to their needs.

2 Provide Digital Content, Tools, & Services

2.1 Increase the Libraries' capacity to create, acquire, and manage digital scholarly content in an increasingly diverse range of formats.

2.2 Facilitate easy, convenient discovery and use of relevant scholarly information.

2.3 Create and refine services to support the use of digital tools and digital content.

2.4 Provide opportunities for staff to become technologically skilled and adaptable.

3 Develop New Research & Teaching Partnerships

3.1 Encourage interaction of Libraries staff with all groups of users, with non-library groups at Duke, with other libraries and with additional organizations to identify opportunities for new collaborations.

3.2 Be an active partner in the development of infrastructure that supports new types of research and publishing.

3.3 Expand Libraries partnerships that serve groups of constituents, such as Duke Engage, services for students studying abroad, and curriculum revision teams.

3.4 Develop a flexible organizational structure and encourage cross-department work.

4 Support University Priorities

4.1 Develop a broad understanding across the Libraries of University priorities.

4.2 Address emerging University priorities in library planning and assessment activities.

4.3 Connect the Libraries with University priorities in our external communications.

5 Enhance Library Spaces

5.1 Complete the Perkins Project, a way of continuing to adapt Libraries spaces to user needs.

5.2 Regularly assess space usage in all Libraries locations and align space planning with evolving user needs.

DUKE UNIVERSITY LIBRARIES

DUKE UNIVERSITY
Improving the User Experience
http://library.duke.edu/about/planning/2010-2012/userexperience.html

Improving the User Experience

Duke Libraries > About Us > Strategic Plan > 2010 - 2012

Improving the User Experience

Understand library users' research and library experiences and use that information to shape collections, spaces, and services.

Strategic Plan 2010-2012

Overview

Strategic Directions

Improve the User Experience

Provide Digital Content, Tools & Services

Develop New Research & Teaching Partnerships

Support University Priorities

Enhance Library Spaces

📄 PDF, entire plan
[23 pages, 76kb]

📄 PDF, 1 pg summary
[1 page, 261kb]

Previous Strategic Plan
(2006-2010)

Activities	Goals

1.1   **Frame a systematic process for collecting and sharing information about the ways library users work.**

- Identify a core team of Libraries staff to guide assessment activities and to design instruments to capture how diverse communities use resources, services, space, the library website and library programs.
- Create a central archive for user data.

1.2   **Use a better understanding of user communities to create extensive and deep collaboration with users at earlier stages of their research and teaching.**

- Participate in LibQual+ Lite
- Create a mechanism for exploring discovery interfaces and other user-centered tools.

1.3   **Institutionalize innovation by employing results from user assessments to improve procedures and services quickly.**

- Experiment with more user-driven collection strategies.
- Develop project management expertise in order to implement projects that respond to user needs and that support emerging research methodologies and data needs.
- Review and pilot an article recommender service to provide information to users regarding the behavior of others who have performed similar searches.

1.4   **Present library programs and services in ways that help users understand the connections to their needs.**

- Have a well defined and well understood service model that describes the similarities and differences across locations.
- Market library services, resources and spaces in ways that match users' communication channels and work styles.

http://library.duke.edu/about/planning/2010-2012/userexperience.html[5/31/11 1:17:51 PM]

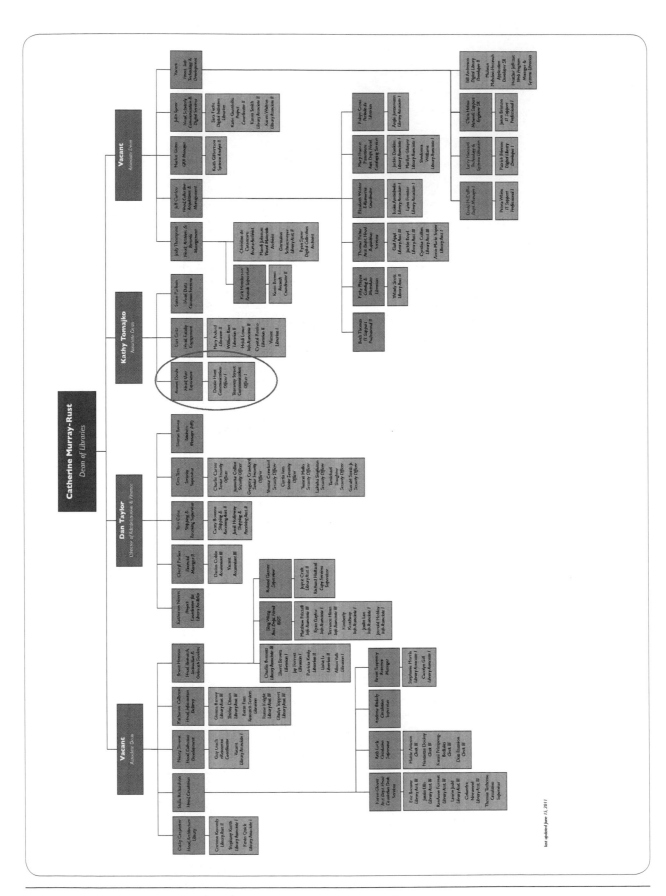

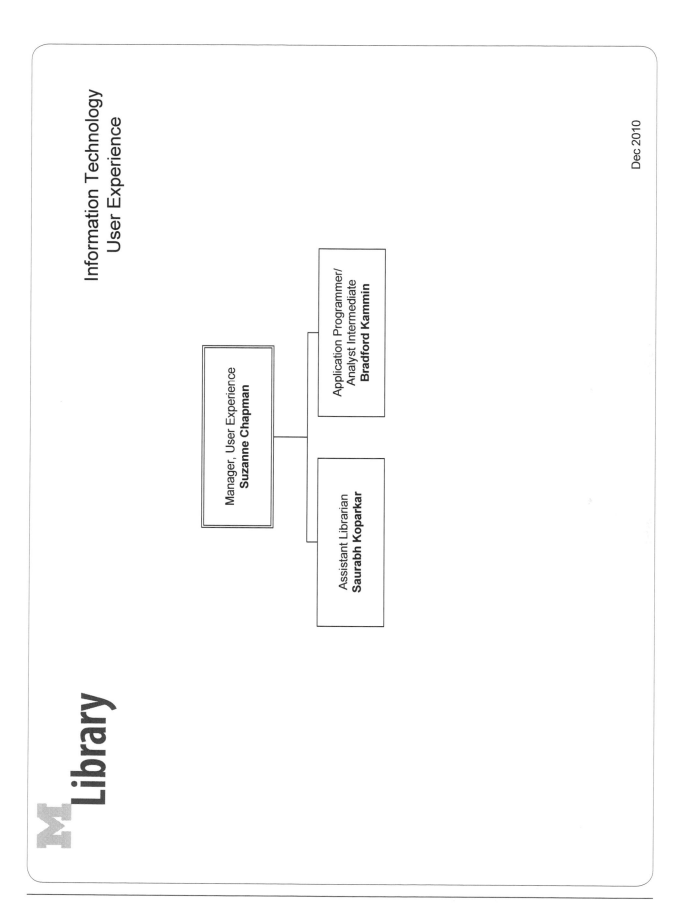

Information Technology
User Experience

Dec 2010

Manager, User Experience
Suzanne Chapman

Application Programmer/
Analyst Intermediate
Bradford Kammin

Assistant Librarian
Saurabh Koparkar

Library

User Experience Projects

Assessment

The UC San Diego library values responsiveness to users and strives to integrate assessment initiatives into service planning & delivery. Using such methods as surveys, usability studies, and statistical analysis, these efforts provide insight into the perceptions, preferences, and needs of library users. The library utilizes these initiatives to predict or effectively respond to the needs of library users and to inform decision-making across operations.

Feedback was recently sought from library users to better understand:

- Student use of Reserve materials
- Functionality and layout of the library's homepage, a newly developed digital asset management system, the UC-wide online catalog, the UC eLinks feature, and select other library web pages
- Ease of navigating the Geisel building
- Satisfaction with interlibrary loan services
- Use of the Scripps Library building
- Faculty use of journals
- Student preferences regarding signage in Geisel

Gathering feedback directly from a wide variety of library users was also a key component of the 2010 development of a new Libraries strategic plan.

Recent analysis of existing data or investigation of library operations has sought to better understand the value and use of:

- Library classrooms
- Navigator Newsletter
- Welcome Week
- A web page targeting new library users
- Document delivery
- RefWorks
- The libraries during various hours
- Various spaces within the Geisel building

The UC San Diego library is committed to serving users as fully as possible within its means and to making regular, sustained efforts to maximize our limited resources.

We welcome suggestions directly from you for areas you think warrant investigation, or on any other library-related issue.

MASSACHUSETTS INSTITUTE OF TECHNOLOGY

Libraries UX Group

https://wikis.mit.edu/confluence/display/LIBUX/Libraries+UX+Group

---

Dashboard › Libraries User Experience Group › Libraries UX Group   Browse ▾   Log In

 Libraries UX Group   ⚙ Tools ▾

Added by Laura Baldwin, last edited by Nicole Gail Hennig on Feb 15, 2011 18:48 (view change)

Libraries UX Group
Nicole Hennig, head

- To email the entire group, use:
  ux-lib@mit.edu✉

- To email the subgroup known as User Interface Group (about web site and virtual interface questions), use this list: uig-lib@mit.edu✉   (Due to the nature of her work, Marion Leeds Carroll is not part of the email lists above).

1. UX Strategy
ux-lib@mit.edu

- Nicole Hennig, lead
- Darcy Duke
- Remlee Green
- Stephanie Hartman
- Lisa Horowitz
- Lisa Sweeney

2. User Interface Group
uig-lib@mit.edu

Send staff questions and requests for work on our our web sites to web-lib@mit.edu. (This list includes Marion).

- Darcy Duke, lead
- Melissa Feiden
- Remlee Green
- Georgiana McReynolds

Web Assistant: Marion Leeds Carroll
Web UI developer: Wendy Bossons

3. UX Public Spaces (a collaborative group that includes members from other areas)

- Nicole Hennig, lead
- Stephanie Hartman, UX
- Lisa Sweeney, SCS
- Millicent Gaskell, CSM
- Keith Glavash, steering committee
- Anita Perkins, SOT
- Cassandra Fox, SOT
- Maria Rodrigues, SOT

We work in the following areas:

(see Area Scoping Form⊗ for more details)

- Assessment: user needs studies, usability testing, surveys of our users' needs, gathering and interpreting stats on use of virtual and physical spaces
- Virtual sites design and production: libraries web site, including all web, mobile and other public-facing interfaces that we can control or customize.

Public spaces: Leading, planning, and assessing design choices for improvements to services in our public spaces, by collaborating with staff at various levels, depending on the scope of the improvement.
- Marketing & communication: Work together with Marketing & Communications area to set the direction for system-wide marketing and communication.

Search this wiki [Search]

- Agenda ideas - UX group
- Announcements from UX
- Apps4Academic planning
- Book covers for displays
- Brainstorm - getting to the next step with userneeds results
- Brainstorm - how to communicate user needs results
- CLIR workshop on faculty research behavior
- Creative Thinking techniques
- Design thinking resources
- Desired Future State
- Device loans to public (Kindle, iPad, etc)
- Device loans to staff (iPad, Kindle, Nook)
- Ebook usability
- Emerging tech hardware list
- Emerging tech subgroup
- Ethnographic research - how to
- iPads
- Lotus blossom diagram
- Meeting task lists
- MIT Libraries new group names
- Morale event ideas
- Organizations and lists
- Projects
- Public spaces UX group
- Scope documents
- Task list - Lisa H
- Task list - Lisa S
- Task list - Stephanie
- User Needs 2006
- User needs studies - past
- User needs study ideas
- User needs study planning - Spring 2011
- UX emergency contact list
- UX FY11 Goals
- UX kickoff meeting
- UX Office Space
- UX Strategy group meeting notes
- UX summit - June 16, 2011

Recruiting Volunteers

Participants needed for library usability study

$15 gift card for one hour of your time

The Libraries IT department is studying new types of library catalog software and how easy this software is to use. Participants are needed to try using the software to find books, find articles, and complete other common library tasks.

Participation takes about an hour and would take place in Norlin Library. You would be given a list of common library tasks to complete while "thinking out loud" about what you are doing. You will also be video-recorded so that we can see exactly when and how the software presents difficulties. Participants will receive a $15 gift card (you can select either Amazon or iTunes) as compensation for your time.

Participants must be current undergraduate students at CU and may not be current or former employees of CU Libraries.

If interested, please contact Rice Majors (rice.majors@colorado.edu) to schedule an appointment.

| Library usability study rice.majors@ colorado.edu | Library usability study rice.majors@ colorado.edu | Library usability study rice.majors@ colorado.edu | Library usability study rice.majors@ colorado.edu | Library usability study rice.majors@ colorado.edu | Library usability study rice.majors@ colorado.edu | Library usability study rice.majors@ colorado.edu | Library usability study rice.majors@ colorado.edu | Library usability study rice.majors@ colorado.edu |

University of Colorado at Boulder Libraries- Research and Instruction Department
Study Title: Card Sort Activity on Library Research Help Guides

Undergraduate Recruitment Text:

In advance:

> Help the Library!
> FREE PIZZA & SNACKS
>
> Are you interested in improving the library's web pages? Could you spare 15-30 minutes to share opinions and ideas about the design and content of research help guides? Pizza and snacks will be offered to participants who help us out.
>
> No prior library research skills are needed but you must be over 18 years of age to participate. Stop by [Rm number] on [date] if you're interested.

On the date:

> TONIGHT- Help the Library!
> FREE PIZZA & SNACKS
>
> Can you spare 15-25 minutes? Pizza and snacks will be offered to participants who come and share opinions and ideas in order to improve the design and content of library research help guides.
>
> No prior library research skills are needed but you must be over 18 years of age to participate. Stop by [Rm number]

Graduate Recruitment Text:

In advance:

Help the Library Help You!

> Can you spare 15minutes? Snacks will be offered to participants who come and share opinions and ideas in order to improve the design and content of library research help guides.
>
> No prior library research skills are needed but you must be over 18 years of age to participate. Stop by [Rm number].
>
> Please stop by room E113 during the following times (TBD) or email caroline.sinkinson@colorado.edu to arrange an appointment.

University of Colorado at Boulder Libraries- Research and Instruction Department
Study Title: Card Sort Activity on Library Research Help Guides

On the date:

Help the Library Help You!

Can you spare 15minutes? Snacks will be offered to participants who come and share opinions and ideas in order to improve the design and content of library research help guides.

No prior library research skills are needed but you must be over 18 years of age to participate. Stop by [Rm number].

Please stop by room E113 during the following times (TBD) : .

Librarian Recruitment Text:

In advance:

Hi Librarians- Help Improve Our Online Help Guides!

Can you spare 15minutes? Snacks will be offered to participants who come and share opinions and ideas in order to improve the design and content of library research help guides.

Please stop by room E113 during the following times (TBD) or email caroline.sinkinson@colorado.edu to arrange an appointment.

On the date:

Hi Librarians- Help Improve Our Online Help Guides!

Can you spare 15minutes? Snacks will be offered to participants who come and share opinions and ideas in order to improve the design and content of library research help guides.

Please stop by room E113 during the following times (TBD) : .

Help improve the Libraries' website.

Spend one hour using and discussing the new *CLIO beta* interface, and receive **$10 cash** for your time.

Email **assessment@columbia.edu** to participate. The study is open April 2010. Space is limited.

Columbia University students, faculty, and staff 18 years of age and older are welcome to participate. This study is approved by the Columbia University IRB, Protocol AAAF0123.

CLIO Beta Usability Test .$10 CASH assessment@columbia. edu	CLIO Beta Usability Test .$10 CASH assessment@columbia. edu	CLIO Beta Usability Test .$10 CASH assessment@columbia. edu	CLIO Beta Usability Test .$10 CASH assessment@columbia. edu	CLIO Beta Usability Test .$10 CASH assessment@columbia. edu	CLIO Beta Usability Test .$10 CASH assessment@columbia. edu	CLIO Beta Usability Test .$10 CASH assessment@columbia. edu	CLIO Beta Usability Test .$10 CASH assessment@columbia. edu	CLIO Beta Usability Test .$10 CASH assessment@columbia. edu	CLIO Beta Usability Test .$10 CASH assessment@columbia. edu

New to the University of Guelph?

Haven't explored the Library yet?

Good.

We're looking for students who are <u>not yet</u> familiar with the Library to walk through the building with us and <u>tell us what you see.</u>

Participants will receive a Hospitality gift card.

For more information please contact:
Robin Bergart   rbergart@uoguelph.ca

Library News

Tex·

Website Usability Study--Participants needed!

Posted: Monday, November 1, 2010

Participants will perform several tasks in Primo, the Library catalogue.

Faculty, grad students and undergraduate students are encouraged to participate.

Usability test will take about 45 minutes and will be conducted in the Library.

No experience with Primo required.

All participants will receive a Chapters gift card.

For more information or to participate in the study please email: libuser@uoguelph.ca

U.Va. student
+ One hour on the Library's website
———————————————————————
= $15 Cavalier Advantage card

Click to find out how to volunteer

UVa Banner Ad for Usability Testing
Fall 2010

This is the text that appeared when the library website banner ad was clicked on.

In an ongoing effort to improve your experience using the Library, we are asking students to volunteer to participate in usability studies to improve our website. The studies will take place in the Science and Engineering usability lab (room 145) and will take approximately one hour. During that hour you will be asked to perform a series of tasks on a portion of the library website. The goal is to improve our site, not to test you. Volunteers will be compensated for their time with a $15 Cavalier Advantage card.

If you are interested in helping the Library please e-mail lib-mis@virginia.edu and you will be contacted about scheduling a time. We will be conducting the first tests October 7th, 2010 but even if you cannot do that date please express your interest and we may call upon you later in the year!

Web Usability

DUKE UNIVERSITY LIBRARIES

Ask Us NOW!

WEB SITE SEARCH: [   ] GO

Hours | Directions | About | Staff

Catalog | Articles | Databases | News

Hours
Directions & Maps
Contact Us
Staff Directory

Libraries
Collections
Departments
Center for
  Instructional
  Technology

News, Events, Exhibits
Projects & Plans
Perkins Renovation
Jobs

Duke Libraries > About Us > Library Assessment > Web Assessment Reports

Web Assessment Reports

* Heatmaps of Key Library Pages: Spring 2011 (March / April 2011)
* Library Website statistics for the 2009-2010 year (July 1, 2009 to June 30, 2010)
* Home Page "Search Resources" Follow-up Presentation - January 13, 2010
* Home Page "Search Resources" Library Presentation - December 16, 2009
* Home Page "Search Resources" tab interface user interview study Report - December 9, 2009
* Home Page Usage: Heatmaps and usage summary for October 11 - 17, 2009

About Web Assessment

Duke University Libraries' Web Interfaces Group (WIG) sponsors regular assessment activities of the Libraries' homepage and supporting pages. This assessment includes, but is not limited to, the following:

1. Public reporting of web statistics via Google Analytics each semester and at the end of the second summer session.

2. User studies in the form of usability studies, circle-mapping, or user interviews of the homepage annually: conducted at the end of the spring semester; analysis and reporting early summer; and changes implemented by start of classes fall semester.

3. User studies in the form of usability studies, user interviews, or focus groups will be conducted on major web interfaces like the Search Resources collective and individual components every year, mid year: analysis and reporting and changes implemented by start of classes fall semester.

4. Content authors will be expected to assess their websites and pages, independently.

The WIG will publish findings and relevant statistics.

Staff from the Libraries' Digital Experience Services department provide assessment-related training and support on the use of Google Analytics and the Libraries' Usability Lab.

Alumni Portal | Divinity School Library | Ford Library | Goodson Law Library | Library Service Center | Lilly Library | Marine Lab Library |
Medical Center Library | Mobile Library (for handheld devices) | Music Library | Perkins/Bostock Library | Special Collections Library | The Link

Use and Reproduction | Privacy | Contact Us | Support the Duke Libraries | Jobs | Duke.edu

ShareThis

(cc) BY-NC-SA

919-660-5870
(Perkins Circulation Desk)

Last modified April 8, 2011 11:17:21 AM EDT

Duke Libraries > About Us > Library Assessment > Web Assessment Reports

Heatmaps of Key Library Pages: Spring 2011

What is this? This page presents heatmaps showing usage trends on several library web pages during spring 2011.

What is a heatmap? Heatmaps are a graphical representation of where patrons clicked when visiting a web page. Cool colors mean fewer clicks, and warm colors mean more clicks.

How did we make heatmaps? We followed steps outlined in the blog post "The definitive heatmap" to create our heatmaps. This method uses javascript, Ruby and RMagick.

Library Homepage: March 21–25

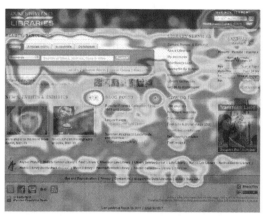

Sample of 40,000 clicks made during the week of March 21, 2011
View large image

Interlibrary Loan page: March 28–30

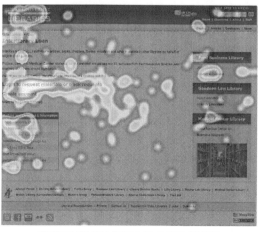

Sample of 500 clicks during week of March 28, 2011
View large image

Special Collections Homepage: April 4–8

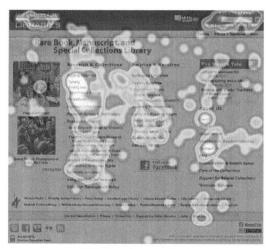

Sample of 800 clicks during week of April 4, 2011
View large image

Data & GIS Homepage: April 11–15

Sample of 230 clicks during week of April 11, 2011
View large image

Music Library home page: April 24–30

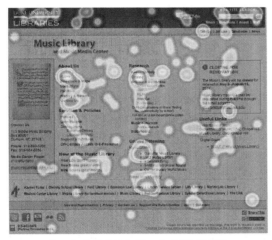

Sample of 300 clicks during week of April 24, 2011
View large image

Alumni Portal | Divinity School Library | Ford Library | Goodson Law Library | Library Service Center | Lilly Library | Marine Lab Library |

Medical Center Library | Mobile Library (for handheld devices) | Music Library | Perkins/Bostock Library | Special Collections Library | The Link

Use and Reproduction | Privacy | Contact Us | Support the Duke Libraries | Jobs | Duke.edu

 ShareThis

919-660-5870
(Perkins Circulation Desk)

Last modified May 2, 2011 9:49:21 AM EDT

MIT   LIBRARIES

User Interface Group

The User Interface Group is a subset of the User Experience Group and serves as the decision-making team for design of the Libraries' public user interfaces. For details, see our charge.

The UIG wiki contains the most up-to-date information about UIG and its activities.

Members

- Darcy Duke, Chair
- Melissa Feiden
- Remlee Green
- Georgiana MacReynolds

User Interface Group

Charge

Membership

Minutes

Projects

Criteria

Resources

Public web
Staff web
MIT

MASSACHUSETTS INSTITUTE OF TECHNOLOGY

User Interface Group. Criteria for prioritizing our work

http://libstaff.mit.edu/uig/criteria.html

M I T   L I B R A R I E S

User Interface Group

Group

Charge

Membership

Minutes

Projects

Criteria

Resources

Public web
Staff web
MIT

User Interface Group

Criteria for prioritizing our work

This list is used for prioritizing the normal, everyday requests and ideas that come our way. It's not for the big projects (i.e. Project SimpLR) that cost extra money and staff time, but just for the everyday work.

User impact

- solves a problem
- affects a large number of users
- things that show we're on the cutting edge
- things that are fun (for us and for users)
- things that have been requested by multiple users (not just one)

Sub-categories of user impact:

- improves known item searching
- improves topical discovery
- improves connections with other systems and tools
- help with evaluating best sources of info
- helps users save time
- helps with personal information management (saving, sorting, sharing, citing what they found)

Staffing

- doesn't take a huge amount of staff time to implement
- things that are easy and we know how to do or could easily find out how to do
- things that we could delegate to students or interns or temp help
- things that don't cost extra money to implement
- improves staff workflow and saves time
- solves more than one problem with one solution

Usability in the Library

About this Site

This website is sponsored by the University of Michigan University Library's Usability Group which is a sub-committee of PARC (Public Access Resource Committee) and ERSC (Electronic Resources Steering Committee). The usability studies represented here have been conducted by various groups throughout the UM Libraries as well as by the Usability Group and its predecessor the Usability Working Group. Only a select group of reports are included here, and more will be added as they are completed.

The goal of this website is to provide open access to our reports and working documents in order to share our findings with the University of Michigan libraries as well as the community-at-large. We hope that sharing our findings will benefit and inform others in their research.

Usability Group Mission Statement

The Usability Group guides and implements usability testing of the Library's web resources and services through short-term task forces comprised of Usability Group members, project stakeholders, and additional volunteers. This includes the Library's locally generated web pages and DLPS (Digital Library Production Service) resources, as well as customizable vendor supported resources, such as MetaLib (SearchTools), Aleph (Mirlyn) and SFX. This group works with PARC and ERSC to set priorities for usability testing shared Library web sites and services, with a focus on testing interfaces and concepts that are broadly implemented across the Library's web environment.

About the Members
Current Members

- Suzanne Chapman (committee chair) - Interface & User Testing Specialist, Digital Library Production Service
- Shevon Desai - Social Science/Humanities Librarian, Reference Department Hatcher Graduate Library
- Kat Hagedorn - Digital Library Projects Manager, Digital Library Production Service
- Julie Piacentine - Public Services Librarian, Reference Department Hatcher Graduate Library
- Ken Varnum - Web Systems Manager, Library Information Technology

Past Members

- David Carter - EECS Librarian; Web & Reference Services Coordinator, Art Architecture & Engineering Library
- Mike Creech - Web Content Manager, MLibrary
- Karen Downing - Foundation & Grants Librarian, Reference Department Hatcher

Graduate Library

- Kat Hagedorn (past committee chair) - Metadata Harvesting Librarian, Digital Library Production Service
- Suzanne Gray - Library Web Services Manager
- Anne Karle-Zenith - Special Projects Librarian, University Library IT & Technical Services
- Shana Kimball - Electronic Projects Editor, Scholarly Publishing Office
- Molly Kleinman - Associate Intellectual Property Specialist and Special Projects Librarian
- Jennifer Nardine - Public Services Librarian, Shapiro Undergraduate Library
- Gurpreet K. Rana - Clinical Education Librarian, Taubman Health Sciences Library
- Bob Tolliver - Engineering Librarian, Art Architecture & Engineering Library

Past Interns

- Jacob Solomon - School of Information (Spring/Summer 2008)
- Matt Schulz - School of Information (Spring/Summer 2008)
- Pratibha Bhaskaran - School of Information (Winter 2008)
- Krystle Williams - School of Information (Winter 2008)
- Julie Piacentine - School of Information (Fall 2007)
- John Suciu - School of Information (Fall 2007)
- Xiaomin Jiang - School of Information (Spring/Summer 2007)
- Josh Morse - School of Information (Spring/Summer 2007)
- Natasha Sant - School of Information (Winter 2007)
- Cora Bledsoe - School of Information (Fall 2006)
- Tonya McCarley - School of Information (Fall 2006)
- Cathy Lu - Web Developer & Analyst, Library Web Services (Spring 2005)
- Kavitha Reddy - School of Information (Spring 2005)

Student Internships

The Usability Working Group sometimes employs student interns from the University of Michigan School of Information. If you are interested in working with us, please contact us for more information.

M Library

About MLibrary   Services   Libraries | MGet It   Search Tools   Catalog (Mirlyn)

UNIVERSITY OF MICHIGAN

Search   GO   Browse   Get Help
                                                      Ask a Librarian   Using the Library

Usability in the Library
Presentations
Projects
Mirlyn (VuFind)
LibGuides
MTagger
MBooks
Library Gateway
Library Websites
SFX
Deep Blue
Search Tools
Resources
Contact

Home > Services > Usability in the Library > Usability in the Library: Mirlyn (VuFind) Reports

Usability in the Library: Mirlyn (VuFind) Reports

About the Project

VuFind is the open-source "next generation" system that has been adapted for use as our new public discovery tool.

Mirlyn "Available Online" Label Guerilla Test (February 2011)

Link to pdf

The goal of this guerilla test was to determine which of four labels (three alternate labels, in addition to the current "available online" label) denoting online availability is preferred by patrons, taking time to ensure that patrons understand the range of situations currently represented by the "available online" label. We also solicited suggestions for alternate labels from participants.

Mirlyn Search Satisfaction Survey (February 2011)

Link to pdf

The primary purpose of this survey was to gather information about how satisfied patrons are with search results in Mirlyn and whether satisfaction levels vary significantly between categories of users (i.e. undergraduates, graduate students, faculty, etc.). The survey was designed to measure satisfaction with searching overall and with two different kinds of searches: known item searches for specific items a patron already knows about and subject searches for items about a particular topic or subject.

VuFind Modified Card Sorting Labels Test (December 2008)

Link to pdf

The goals for this test were to solicit suggestions from users for labeling facet categories, determine how users perceive the relative importance of facets, and determine how many narrowing terms users would like to see within each facet.

VuFind Look-n-Feel Guerilla Test (November 2008)

Link to pdf

The goal for this test was to evaluate how users perceive the catalog when it is and is not embedded into a page with navigation tool bars located at the top of the library's homepage.

VuFind Login Guerilla Test (November 2008)

Link to pdf | Link to pdf of test data

The goal for this test was to determine how users perceive login when using the catalog, and at which access points it is best to force a login decision.

Page maintained by khage
Last modified: 02/08/2011

Facility Design

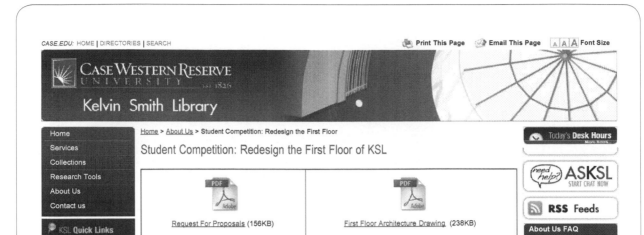

CASE.EDU: HOME | DIRECTORIES | SEARCH

Print This Page   Email This Page   A A A Font Size

CASE WESTERN RESERVE
UNIVERSITY est 1826

Kelvin Smith Library

- Home
- Services
- Collections
- Research Tools
- About Us
- Contact us

KSL Quick Links
- My Library Account
- Find Articles
- Ask A Librarian
- Catalog
- Course Reserves
- OhioLINK
- Copyright@Case

KSL News Blog

May 24, 2011
Refreshed Interface on OhioLINK Catalog
Small changes can make a big difference for you when you search & locate items or request them on th...

May 23, 2011
Discover the Freely Available Yale Digital Commons
Yale increased its impact and access this month with its announcement of free use, without license, ...

May 18, 2011
Text KSL!
Are you away from campus this summer? KSL can help you find a book, journal, paper, and more. Just t...

May 12, 2011
Summer Hours @KSL
Summer hours are in effect at KSL, and we're open 6 days a week for you to come in and work, study, ...

RSS

Other Blogs
KSL Reference & Instruction
ITS News

Home > About Us > Student Competition: Redesign the First Floor

Student Competition: Redesign the First Floor of KSL

PDF — Request For Proposals (156KB)

PDF — First Floor Architecture Drawing (238KB)

Today's Desk Hours

ASKSL START CHAT NOW

RSS Feeds

About Us FAQ
What and Where is Siegal?
View All FAQs

Floor Layouts (PDF's):
- Lower Level
- First Floor
- Second Floor
- Third Floor

Overview

Kelvin Smith Library (KSL) is sponsoring a competition for student teams to redesign the entire first floor in an effort to transform the KSL into a vibrant intellectual community center for campus learning and research. Students are invited to create teams that will: (1) study the needs of undergraduate and graduate students and faculty, (2) develop a basis of design and program plan, and (3) present the proposed plan to an expert panel for review.

Proposals will be evaluated by the Evaluation Panel based upon the creativity, cost-effectiveness, practicality, and sustainability of the proposals. The number of prizes awarded may vary depending upon the total number of submissions. First prize will be $2,500 to the team.

Teams should consider which services, functions, or features should be added, redesigned, moved to other floors, or eliminated entirely. Proposed designs should complement and enhance the aesthetics of the building, and ensure that KSL is a warm and inviting environment that has a logical layout of features. Teams may choose to change, augment or maintain the current color palette, add artwork or display spaces, add dynamic visual display panels, and change or improve signage. The team also should recommend changes to the furniture. The only parameters for the redesign are: (1) the space for the new library cafe is assigned but the area can be proposed for redesign; (b) any proposed changes to the compact shelving must be accompanied by an alternative onsite location for an equivalent number of volumes; and (3) no relocation can occur to load bearing walls, elevators or restrooms.

Proposal Contents

- **Research findings** concerning library-related learning and research needs of undergraduate and graduate students and of faculty, including best practices and team survey or focus groups results.
- **Strategic program outline**, including the major organizational, functional, economic, and aesthetic goals for the redesign, environmental sustainability opportunities, accessibility for persons with disabilities, the flexibility of the design for future modification, expected capacity and traffic flow, and the potential for implementing the design in phases.
- **Detailed program plan and design**, including a written report, diagrams of the floor with adjacencies of the different functions, the preferred footprint for each of the major functions, major site requirements, and known constraints or obstacles.

Process

Timeframe and Deadlines. [Note: the following dates are tentative and subject to change]

- ~~Pre-proposal informational meetings: December 2, 2010 at 10:00 am; January 12, 2011 at 10:00 am; January 20, 2011 at 2:00 pm~~

* *Statement of Intent to Submit a Proposal*: January 21, 2011 (no later than noon)
* *Library staff available for group interview sessions*: January 21, 2011 (noon)
* *Final written submission*: March 14, 2011 (5:00 pm)
* *Team Presentations to Evaluation Panel* [open university forum]: TBD (March 21 – 31)
* *Awards announced*: April 11, 2011

Student Competition: Redesign the First Floor of Kelvin Smith Library

Request for Proposals (RFP) – Issue Date: 16 November 2010

Kelvin Smith Library (KSL) is sponsoring a competition for student teams to redesign the entire first floor in an effort to transform the KSL into a vibrant intellectual community center for campus learning and research. Students are invited to create teams that will: (1) study the needs of undergraduate and graduate students and faculty, (2) develop a basis of design and program plan, and (3) present the proposed plan to an expert panel for review. Proposals will be evaluated by the Evaluation Panel based upon the creativity, cost-effectiveness, practicality, and sustainability of the proposals. The number of prizes awarded may vary depending upon the total number of submissions. First prize will be $2,500 to the team.

Teams should consider which services, functions, or features should be added, redesigned, moved to other floors, or eliminated entirely. Proposed designs should complement and enhance the aesthetics of the building, and ensure that KSL is a warm and inviting environment that has a logical layout of services and features. Particular attention should be paid to the following:

- **Functions**. Within the limitations outlined below, the entire floor is eligible for redesign. Teams should consider which services, functions, or features should be added to the floor, which current service points should be redesigned, and which functions or services should be eliminated entirely or shifted or moved to other floors.

- **Aesthetics**. The design should complement and enhance the aesthetics of the building, while also enhancing the environment to ensure that KSL is a warm and inviting place to be with a logical arrangement of functions. To accomplish this, the teams may choose to recommend changes to the current color palette, add artwork, create new community spaces (such as artwork), add visual signage or display panels, change or improve signage, etc.

- **Furnishings**. The team should recommend appropriate furniture to accomplish the functions that will be housed on the first floor. For any new furnishings, design ideas using commercially-available furniture should be included in the proposal as examples. [See Appendix for examples of some potential providers of furnishings.]

- **Parameters.**
  - Over the next few months KSL will undertaking some pilot projects that will result in temporary changes to the first floor and that will open up the space. Teams may choose to incorporate or ignore these changes.
  - Space is reserved for a new library café that will open soon. While adequate space to accommodate this café must be included in the design plan, the team is invited to recommend design changes that would complement or enhance the community area created by the café.
  - It is desirable, but not required, that the compact shelving currently on the first floor should remain in position. Proposals to reduce or eliminate this shelving must identify a suitable alternative to provide onsite access to an equivalent number of volumes.
  - The team cannot recommend relocation of load bearing walls, elevators or restrooms.

1

- **Research.** The team should conduct and report upon its research findings concerning library-related the learning and research needs of undergraduate and graduate students and of faculty. To identify critical, highly desirable, and desirable space needs, this research may include the following.

  1. Ascertaining current best practices as reported by CWRU's peer and aspirational institutions on the web, in the literature, or through direct contact.

  2. Gathering primary research results from information gathered directly by the team about the activities, schedules, and needs of the CWRU community (e.g., through surveys, focus groups and interviews). Teams may contact faculty, students, university administrators, or other staff for interviews[1], but teams may interview library staff <u>only</u> in group sessions that the library will hold on dates shown in "Timeframes and Deadlines" section below. Formal or informal interviews of library staff outside of these meetings may result in a team being disqualified.

- **Strategic program outline.** Based upon its research, the proposal should outline the major organizational, functional, economic, and aesthetic goals for the redesign. Specific issues the proposal should address include: (1) environmental sustainability issues and opportunities, (2) issues of accessibility by persons with disabilities, (3) services functions that should be centralized or decentralized, (3) the flexibility of the design for future modification (especially to accommodate new technologies), (5) expected building capacity and flow of traffic, and (6) the potential for implementing the design in phases. Although estimates of specific construction costs are not required, the proposal should provide sufficient information to demonstrate that the design can be achieved at a reasonable cost.

- **Detailed Program Plan and Design.** Although technical architectural drawings are not required, the final proposal must provide floorplans in sufficient detail to illustrate the preferred footprint for each of the major functions, the adjacencies of the various functions, major site requirements, and known constraints or obstacles. The proposal must include scale drawings of the first floor space, but architectural renderings (views, 3-D models, electrical or other wiring schematics) welcome but not required.

PROCESS

- **Academic Credit.** It is permissible for teams or individual team members to earn academic credit for participation in this project, but students who wish to do are entirely responsible for identifying faculty, and those faculty are governed solely by that faculty member. Such faculty may establish requirements for earning academic credit that are in addition to those outlined in this RFP.

---

[1] Any such primary research must comply with CWRU regulations concerning research with human subjects.

2

- **Timeframe and Deadlines. [Note: the following dates are tentative and subject to change]**

  o Pre-proposal meetings: December 2, 2010 at 10:00 am; January 12, 2011 at 10:00; January 20, 2011 at 2:00 pm. These sessions are to answer questions student teams may have. All questions and answers will be summarized and made available to all teams that submit a "Statement of Intent" [see below].

  o Statement of Intent to Submit a Proposal: January 21, 2011 (due no later than noon). It is a requirement that any team that plans to submit a proposal must submit this Statement of Intent by the deadline. Failure to do so will lead to disqualification. The statement is simply to indicate that the team plans to submit a proposal, and should include the names, college affiliation and email addresses of each the expected team members. No pre-proposal information is expected from teams at this time, and the team is free to withdraw its proposal or change the names of team members at a later date.

  o Library staff group interview sessions. Note: the staff who attend each session may vary.
    - January 24 at 2:00 pm
    - February 8 at 10:30 am
    - February 14 at 2:00 pm
    - March 3 at 11:00 am

  o Final written submission: March 14, 2011 at 5:00 pm. All proposal must be submitted electronically to the Associate Provost and University Librarian (Arnold.hirshon@case.edu)

  o Team Presentations to Evaluation Panel. Presentations will be open (as space permits) to all members of the university community. The actual date of the presentations is to be determined, but will likely occur between March 21 and March 31, 2011

  o Awards announced: April 11, 2011

REQUIREMENTS

- **Team Composition.** All final submissions must be the result of the work of a team collaborative that includes two or more team members.   Diversity among team members is desirable but not required, e.g., representation with a team by different disciplines or colleges, inclusion of graduate and undergraduate students, multiple generations, different cultural backgrounds, etc. Team members must be currently enrolled students at CWRU[2].

- **Health and Safety.** Designs should comply with general university health and safety requirements, as well as university rules and regulations for conducting social science research with human subjects.

---

[2] Students of other University Circle higher education institutions (e.g., Cleveland Institute of Art, Cleveland Institute of Music) may participate as team members providing the predominant number of members of that team are students currently enrolled at CWRU.

3

EVALUATION

- **Criteria.** Proposals will be evaluated by the Evaluation Panel based upon the creativity, cost-effectiveness, practicality, and sustainability of the proposals.

- **Evaluation Panel.** The composition of the evaluation panel will be announced at a later time. The panel will include a broad representation of expertise and perspectives from both within and outside of the university community. Once announced, team members are prohibited from contacting panel members (informally or formally) for purposes of gathering information directly related to this RFP.

AWARD

There must be at least two (2) teams that submit proposals for any prizes to be awarded. The total number of prizes awarded will not exceed N+1 of the number of submissions, e.g., there must be at least three (3) qualifying teams for the granting of a second prize, etc. No more than three (3) prizes will be awarded.

- First Prize $ 2,500 to the team
- Second Prize $1,500 to the team
- Third Prize $ 750 to the team

CAVEATS

By submitting a proposal, all team members must agree to the following:
- KSL reserves the right to suspend the competition if there are not at least two qualifying teams, and to notify any teams that may have submitted or intended to submit a proposal.
- The Evaluation Panel may disqualify any proposals that do not comply with the specifications of this RFP
- Teams must agree that the intellectual property of all submissions becomes a property of Case Western Reserve University, and that the submissions, in whole or in part, may be made available through a Creative Commons license.
- Teams must agree that KSL may use any ideas from any teams (regardless of whether the team received an award) without providing any remuneration other than that specified under the Award section of this RFP.
- No guarantee is implied that program plans will be used in their entirety or in part by KSL.

QUESTIONS

Any questions about this competition or the contents of this RFP that are not asked during one of the pre-proposal informational meetings must be directed in writing to Arnold Hirshon, Associate Provost and University Librarian (arnold.hirshon@case.edu). Answers will be shared with all teams that have filed a Statement of Intent.

4

Appendix

1. **Examples of Suppliers of Library Furnishings**

http://www.brodartfurniture.com/

http://www.highsmith.com/?CID=HG1000LIBRARYSUPPLIESHP&gclid=CMCpkPWT86QCFWQz5wod3hL8jg

http://www.gaylord.com/listing.asp?H=23

2. **Sample Statement of Intent**

Send this statement of intent to: Arnold.hirshon@case.edu by no later than noon on January 21, 2011.

The individuals listed below plan to submit as a team a proposal for the Student Competition to Redesign the First Floor of Kelvin Smith Library.   We understand that:

- It is a requirement that any team that plans to submit a proposal must submit this Statement of Intent by the deadline, and that failure to do so will lead to disqualification.
- The statement is simply to indicate that our team plans to submit a proposal.
- Our team is free to withdraw its proposal or change the names of team members at a later date.

Team Member	College or School	Email

5

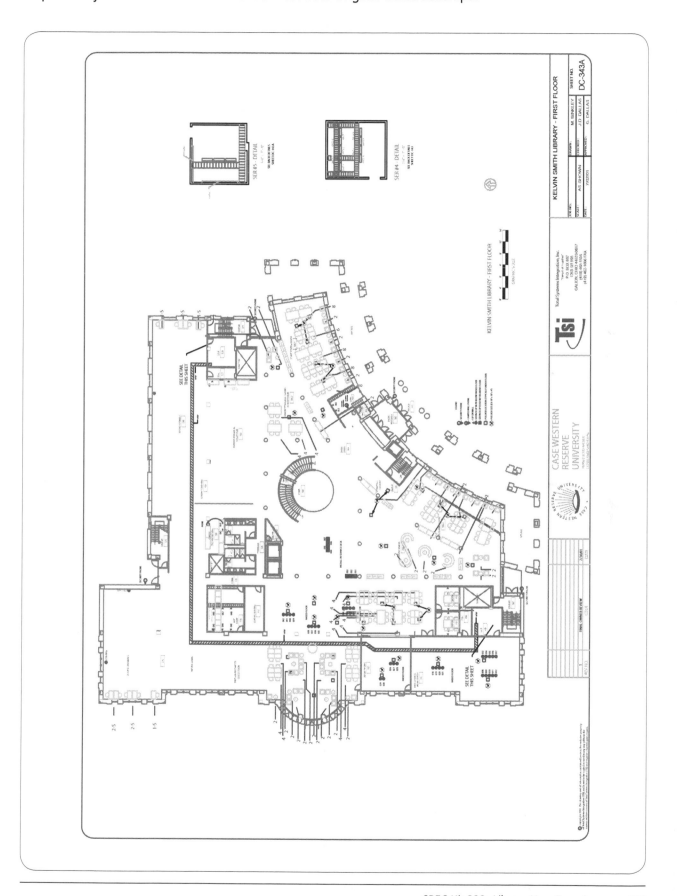

The Joe and Rika Mansueto Library
Grand Reading Room
Lighting and Laptop Survey

Directions: The chair and table on display here have been selected for the Mansueto Library Grand Reading Room, and lighting and laptop lock fixtures are now being considered. Please have a seat and answer the questions below. (Circle your answer where options are provided.)

1. Evaluate the light cast by the horizontal fluorescent bulb.   Too dim   Good   Too bright

2. Do you expect to use a laptop in the Grand Reading Room?   Yes   No
   A. If so, would you use the bar near the outlets to secure your
      computer to the table?   Yes   No
      1. If so, is the location of the bar appropriate?   Yes   No
         a. If not, please suggest a better position.

3. Do you have any additional comments? (Use reverse side.)

4. About you: Faculty   Grad/prof. student   College student
                  Library staff   Other university staff   Other: _____

5. If you would like to be notified about final lighting and laptop decisions, please provide your:

   Name_____   E-mail _____

Thank you for your participation. Please deposit the completed survey in the box on the table.

The Joe and Rika Mansueto Library
Grand Reading Room Rendering for
Lighting and Laptop Survey

The table and chair on display here are part of a set that will be used in the Mansueto Library Grand Reading Room, as depicted in the rendering below.

In addition to the fluorescent lighting on the tables, fixtures (only some of which are depicted here) will provide light from above, and there will be natural light during the daytime.

 mansueto.lib.uchicago.edu

: : Home >> 2 West

West Commons (LWC)
Productivity Cluster
Multimedia Studio
Rehearsal Studio
Information Services

East Commons (LEC)
Group Computing
Performance Space
Circulation
Exhibits
Jazzman's Cafe

Technology Support Center
OIT@Technology Support Center
Multipurpose Room

2 West
Renovation

About the Commons
History
Reactions
Project Documents
Photos

GT Library

Welcome to 2 West!

We hope you will enjoy using the newly renovated 2 West. Please use the space and tell us what you like or do not like by **submitting your feedback**.

▸ **Recent photos of 2 West:**

 More info? Contact:

Ameet Doshi
User Engagement Librarian and
Assessment Coordinator
Phone: 404-894-4598

(Photos by Dottie Hunt, GT Library)

Throughout the planning and design process, students provided a wealth of feedback about how the space should look and feel. Below, you will find a number of documents related to the user-driven design of 2 West. Thanks to everyone who participated and please contact us with more suggestions and feedback - we would like to hear from you.

▸ **Design concepts:**
   REVIEW the layouts & SHARE your thoughts!

▸ **Renovation Message Boards:**

Share your ideas about different aspects of the 2 West space.

- Atmosphere
- Furniture
- Work Flow & Function
- Supplies, Equipment, & Technology

▸ **Research and Presentations:**

2 West Final Draft

What should we do with 2 West?
by Brian Mathews, May 2008

2 West Space Demos for Focus Groups
by Brian Mathews

2 West Focus Group Space Photos Response Sheet

2 West Affinity Group Results
Spring 2008

2 West Design Charrette Instruction Sheet
Winter 2009

2 West Design Charrette Time Lapse Video

2 West Findings

▸ **Technique Articles:**

Library finds funding for renovations
January 16, 2009

How can the Library be improved? and What would you change in the Library second floor?
February 29, 2008

Library plans new renovations
February 22, 2008

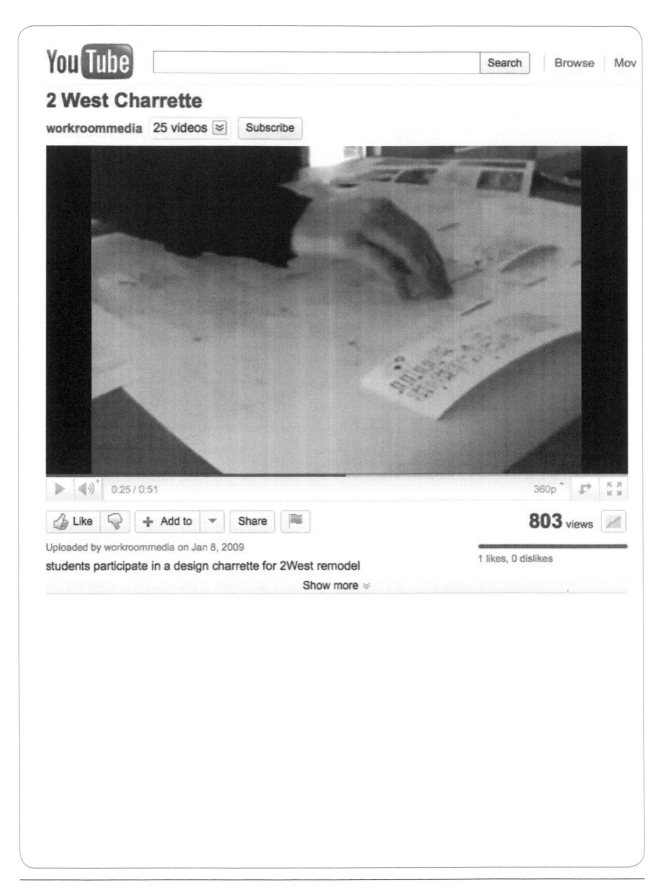

Outreach

GEORGIA TECH
"Lost in the Stacks" on WREK Radio
http://lostinthestacks.org

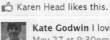 **"Lost in the Stacks" on WREK Radio** 👍 Like

Education

Wall · "Lost in the Stacks" on W... · **Top Posts** ▼

- 📺 **Wall**
- Info
- Photos
- Notes
- Links
- Video

About

Georgia Tech's Research Library Rock n Roll Radio Show on WREK 91.1 FM Atla...

More

578
people like this

Likes   See All

 Sound Opinions

 Archbishop Marsh's Library

 This I Believe at Tech

 Robert C. Williams Paper Museum

 Digital Library of Georgia

Create a Page
Report Page
Share

 "Lost in the Stacks" on WREK Radio

Playlist for Friday, May 27th ("This I Believe")

"Horn Intro" by Modest Mouse "Friction" by Television "This I Believe Introduction" by Edward R. Murrow (clip) "M. Daguerre" by Rachel's (background)...

🔲 May 27 at 2:29pm · Like · Comment

👍 Karen Head likes this.

 Kate Godwin I loved this show, y'all!
May 27 at 9:30pm

📕 **"Lost in the Stacks" on WREK Radio** Thank you, Kate!
Saturday at 5:59am

 **"Lost in the Stacks" on WREK Radio**
is excited to offer you a new and experimental show today! "This I Believe" will include interviews with Dana Hartley, Pete Ludovice, and Brian Dyke, along with audio from This I Believe at Tech winners. You'll also hear music from Toadies, Queen, Jenny Lewis, and plenty more. Tune in to 91.1FM in Atlanta or stream that sucker from wrek.org wor

 WREK Atlanta, 91.1 FM | quality, diverse programming
www.wrek.org

WREK is the entirely student managed, operated and engineered radio station at Georgia Tech. We broadcast 24/7 on 91.1 FM with 40,000 Watts of quality, diverse programming.

🔗 May 27 at 5:35am · Like · Comment

👍 Dana Hartley, Grant Jerkins and 2 others like this.

 Dana Hartley Great job! My whole family and I listened during breakfast – yes, breakfast...
May 27 at 2:19pm · 👍 1 person

 "Lost in the Stacks" on WREK Radio
has put together a special edition for tomorrow: WREK 91.1 FM is our laboratory!

May 26 at 7:03am · Like · Comment

👍 Jj O'Brien and Kasie Keith Bennett like this.

"Lost in the Stacks" on WREK Radio added 2 new photos to the album

Sign Up **Facebook helps you connect and share with the people in your life.**

facebook

"The 'Public' Library."

"The 'Public' Library"

 May 24 at 1:23pm · Like · Comment

 Parul Parikh and Ed Martin like this.

> **"Lost in the Stacks" on WREK Radio** hear the streaming archive of this show for one week! http://wrek.org /fridayshows
> May 24 at 1:24pm

 Toral Shah Doshi
"Warning: Historical recordings may contain offensive language."

 National Jukebox LOC.gov
www.loc.gov
The Library of Congress presents the National Jukebox, which makes historical sound recordings available to the public free of charge. The Jukebox includes recordings from the extraordinary collections of the Library of Congress Packard Campus for Audio Visual Conservation and other contributing lib

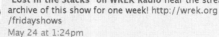 May 11 at 6:14am · Like · Comment

 Raj Chakraberti likes this.

 "Lost in the Stacks" on WREK Radio

> **Playlist for Friday, May 20th ("The Public Library")**
> Intro: "Friction" by Television   "Everybody's Gonna Be Happy" by Queens of the Stone Age   F...

May 24 at 8:54am · Like · Comment

 Ed Martin likes this.

> **"Lost in the Stacks" on WREK Radio** It was our pleasure!
> May 26 at 7:40am

 "Lost in the Stacks" on WREK Radio
is pleased to offer you a new show today at noon EDT! "The Public Library" will focus on public programming in the Georgia Tech Library and includes music from The Who, Two Door Cinema Club, and plenty more. Tune in to 91.1FM in Atlanta, or stream that sucker on wrek.org worldwide.

 WREK Atlanta, 91.1 FM | quality, diverse programming
wrek.org
WREK is the entirely student managed, operated and engineered radio station at Georgia Tech. We broadcast 24/7 on 91.1 FM with 40,000 Watts of quality, diverse programming.

May 20 at 5:54am · Like · Comment

Chelsea Hopper likes this.

Maria Sotnikova New Socks?!?!?!
May 20 at 7:15am

HesburghLibraries
UNIVERSITY OF NOTRE DAME

Senior Thesis Camp

Fall Break 2010—Hesburgh Library, Lower Level

The program is designed to assist seniors who are writing theses in Arts & Letters. Students will have the opportunity to jumpstart the research and writing process by working in dedicated spaces in the library and by consulting with librarians and writing tutors about their work. The program will help students establish a framework for writing and research that will enable them to work effectively. Through informal conversations and short presentations of their research, they will also develop a sense of community with other students. Members of the Center for Undergraduate Scholarly Engagement will talk about the annual research fair and opportunities for graduate study. Each day the library will provide breakfast and refreshments and there will be a lunch on the final day to celebrate the completion of the program.

Students

> Provide the name of their advisor
> Provide a brief description of their research interests
> Provide some basic information on their familiarity with library research

Librarians

> Conduct a workshop on research essentials
> Conduct a workshop on literature reviews
> Conduct a workshop on formatting citations with RefWorks
> Provide research consultations for individual students
> Provide subject specific workshops (depending on participants)
> Provide a brief presentation on the Library Research Award

Writing Center

> Conduct a workshop on writing essentials
> Provide individual consultations for students

CUSE

> Conduct a presentation on research opportunities, graduate fellowships and funding
> Conduct a presentation on preparing for the Undergraduate Scholars Conference

Arts & Letters Advisors

> Encourage students to enroll
> Meet with students before and after to check progress

CONTACT
Cheri Smith
Coordinator for Instructional Services
csmith@nd.edu
631-4271

Hesburgh Libraries
University of Notre Dame

UNIVERSITY OF NOTRE DAME
Senior Thesis Camp

Tentative schedule:

Monday, October 18th

9:00-9:30	Continental breakfast
9:30-10:00	Introductions and library research essentials
10:00-3:00	Writing time/*Individual consultations by appointment*
3:00	Refreshments/Review of the first day

Tuesday, October 19th

9:00-9:30	Continental breakfast
9:30-10:00	Writing Center presentation
10:00-3:00	Writing time/*Individual consultations by appointment*
3:00	Refreshments/Library Research Award

Wednesday, October 20th

9:00-9:30	Continental breakfast
9:30-10:30	Literature Review Workshop
10:30-3:00	Writing time/*Individual consultations by appointment*
3:00	Refreshments/CUSE—Undergraduate Scholars Conference, and opportunities for graduate work and postgraduate fellowships

Thursday, October 21st

9:00-9:30	Continental breakfast
9:30-10:30	RefWorks
10:30-3:00	Writing time/*Individual consultations by appointment*
3:00	Refreshments

Friday, October 22nd

9:00-9:30	Continental breakfast
9:30-12:00	Student presentations (brief) on progress, problems, etc.
12:00-1:00	Lunch

Hesburgh Libraries
University of Notre Dame

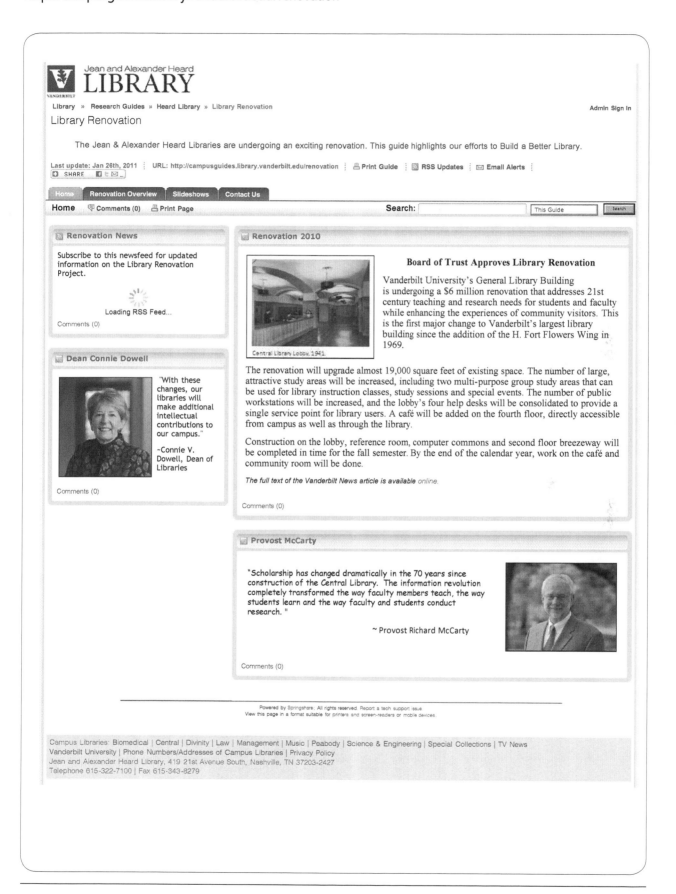

Jean and Alexander Heard
LIBRARY
VANDERBILT

Library » Research Guides » Heard Library » Library Renovation

Admin Sign In

Library Renovation

The Jean & Alexander Heard Libraries are undergoing an exciting renovation. This guide highlights our efforts to Build a Better Library.

Last update: Jan 26th, 2011 | URL: http://campusguides.library.vanderbilt.edu/renovation | 🖨 Print Guide | 🔊 RSS Updates | ✉ Email Alerts |
🔗 SHARE ...

| Home | Renovation Overview | Slideshows | Contact Us |

Home   💬 Comments (0)   🖨 Print Page

Search: [_____] [This Guide ▾] [Search]

🔲 Renovation News

Subscribe to this newsfeed for updated information on the Library Renovation Project.

Loading RSS Feed...

Comments (0)

🔲 Dean Connie Dowell

"With these changes, our libraries will make additional intellectual contributions to our campus."

~Connie V. Dowell, Dean of Libraries

Comments (0)

🔲 Renovation 2010

Central Library Lobby, 1941.

Board of Trust Approves Library Renovation

Vanderbilt University's General Library Building is undergoing a $6 million renovation that addresses 21st century teaching and research needs for students and faculty while enhancing the experiences of community visitors. This is the first major change to Vanderbilt's largest library building since the addition of the H. Fort Flowers Wing in 1969.

The renovation will upgrade almost 19,000 square feet of existing space. The number of large, attractive study areas will be increased, including two multi-purpose group study areas that can be used for library instruction classes, study sessions and special events. The number of public workstations will be increased, and the lobby's four help desks will be consolidated to provide a single service point for library users. A café will be added on the fourth floor, directly accessible from campus as well as through the library.

Construction on the lobby, reference room, computer commons and second floor breezeway will be completed in time for the fall semester. By the end of the calendar year, work on the café and community room will be done.

The full text of the Vanderbilt News article is available online.

Comments (0)

🔲 Provost McCarty

"Scholarship has changed dramatically in the 70 years since construction of the Central Library. The information revolution completely transformed the way faculty members teach, the way students learn and the way faculty and students conduct research. "

~ Provost Richard McCarty

Comments (0)

Powered by Springshare; All rights reserved. Report a tech support issue.
View this page in a format suitable for printers and screen-readers or mobile devices.

Campus Libraries: Biomedical | Central | Divinity | Law | Management | Music | Peabody | Science & Engineering | Special Collections | TV News
Vanderbilt University | Phone Numbers/Addresses of Campus Libraries | Privacy Policy
Jean and Alexander Heard Library, 419 21st Avenue South, Nashville, TN 37203-2427
Telephone 615-322-7100 | Fax 615-343-8279

User Feedback

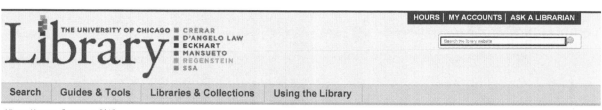

HOURS | MY ACCOUNTS | ASK A LIBRARIAN

Search the library website

| Search | Guides & Tools | Libraries & Collections | Using the Library |

Library Home > Surveys > 2010

Survey of graduate and professional school students

RESULTS:

- Survey report
- Respondent comments
- Library response to results
- Summary results
- Survey form

What is the 2010 Survey of graduate and professional students?
The 2010 Survey of Professional and Graduate Students, which ran from February 9-15, 2010, launched the University of Chicago Library's new annual survey program which will target, on a rotating basis, graduate students, faculty, and undergraduates.

What does the survey cover?
The 23-question survey, designed by the Assessment Project Team and based on similar surveys run by MIT and the University of Washington, covered:
- Demographic information: division/school, degree program, whether respondents were in first year at University
- Collections: importance, satisfaction, impact on success , comments/suggestions
- Activities: physical/remote visits, activities when visiting library, website tasks
- Spaces: primary library, library satisfaction, frequency of visits , comments/suggestions
- Existing services/facilities: importance, satisfaction, comments/suggestions
- New services: importance of services presented as options, top pick, comments/suggestions
- Overall satisfaction

Who took the survey?
- Invitations were sent to 9,726 graduate and professional school students who were enrolled in a degree program
- 1,791 students completed the survey, yielding an 18% response rate
- The highest number of responses (423) came from the Social Sciences Division and the Humanities Division (303), which together account for 41% of the completed surveys.
- Degree programs: 62% (934) Doctoral degree, 37% (657) Masters degree, around 5% are in Law or Medical degrees

What are the 2010 survey results?
Results include (see the full report for detailed analysis):
- 93% report that they are either very satisfied or satisfied with the Library overall
- 92% rate electronic journals and magazines as either very important or important to their current research and study
- 85% report being very satisfied or satisfied with our collection of electronic journals and magazines
- 86% rate the Library's collections as either very important or important when it comes to their effectiveness as a researcher
- 76% report accessing the Library resources from off campus at least weekly
- Among the proposed services that participants rated as important to offer were scanning and online delivery of print journal articles, and designated quiet zones
- Over 4,000 coded comments in response to the 6 open-ended questions highlight the reliance on electronic access and collections and the importance to many of the Library as work space.

How is the Library responding to these results?
In addition to responses to specific requests, both the quantitative and qualitative data are reviewed and acted on by various committees and workgroups, including:
- The Library Planning Council will use the results to develop priorities for the next fiscal year
- Results will be reviewed and acted on by the Public Services Steering Committee, the Virtual Access Committee, and the Web Improvement Team.

Assessment Project Team members: Agnes Tatarka, Assessment Director; David Larsen, Head of Access Services and Assessment: Tod Olson, Systems Librarian; Margaret Schilt, D'Angelo Law Library Faculty Services Librarian; Andrea Twiss-Brooks, Co-Director, John Crerar Library

The University of Kansas Libraries

Libraries Home

Articles & Databases

Catalog: books & more

E-journals

Research by Subject

Course Reserves

Library Pages A-Z

Images

KU ScholarWorks

» more Digital Collections

Hours

My Account

Request Materials

Friends & Benefactors

Suggestions

Snapshot Day at Anschutz Library, April 14, 2010

What is a day in the life of Anschutz Library like? From the bustling Group Study areas to the cloister like quiet zones, Anschutz is a veritable hive of activity. Patrons at Anschutz are in the midst of a variety of activities, from searching for jobs to studying for finals at any given time.

On April 14th, KU Libraries joined Kansas Libraries in documenting SnapShot Day: A Day in the Life of a Kansas Library. Snapshot Day was an effort to document the importance of libraries in their communities. Patron surveys were conducted to find the variety of reasons why hundreds of people walk through the doors of Anschutz each day.

Patrons on Snapshot Day were asked what resources they were using as well as their likes and suggestions for bettering service in Anschutz.to see the survey results.

- View the graph detailing services used
- View the response sheet
- Click through the photo gallery

For more information about KU Libraries, visit http://www.lib.ku.edu/pressroom/.

View the snapshots from Snapshot Day

Click to view full-sized images

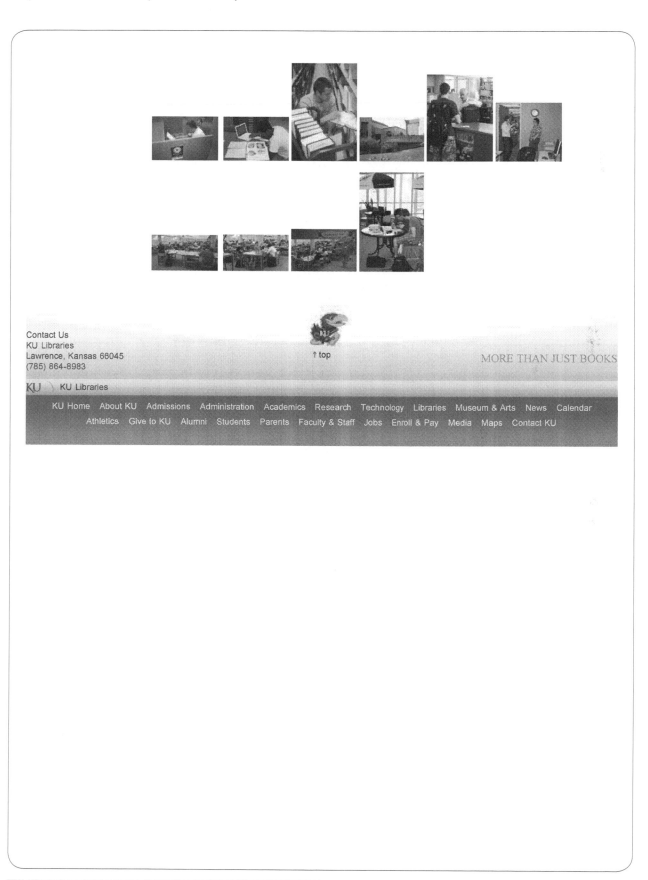

Dashboard › Libraries User Experience Group › Libraries UX Group   Browse ▾ Log In

› User needs study planning - Spring 2011

› Ethnographic study - Digital Scholarship at MIT

 Ethnographic study - Digital Scholarship   ⚙ Tools ▾

at MIT

Added by Nicole Gail Hennig, last edited by Lisa Horowitz on Apr 21, 2011 13:02 (view change)

Digital Scholarship at MIT

Team: Nicole, Remlee, Stephanie, Lisa H; Michelle Baildon, Anne Graham, Kate McNeill

Timeline

Email communications to users: recruiting, informing of selection (or not), reminder, scheduling

Interview schedule (restricted)

Classes and Projects Involved (restricted)

Interview Training

Interview brain dump (restricted)

Coding

Proposal

Digital Scholarship at MIT:
a study of how new technologies and formats are changing how MIT scholars find and use information

Goal:

The MIT Libraries User Needs group studies the needs of the MIT community in order to inform the future of library services for MIT. In the Spring of 2011 we propose to study how new technologies and formats are having an impact on how MIT scholars find, use, and share information for their study, research, and publishing. This will help inform our work related to the following strategic directions:

- Create the Next Generation Research Library Organization
- Build and Strengthen Relationships with Faculty, Students, and the MIT Community
- Advocacy for Information Policy
- Improve Infrastructure for Content Management and Delivery
- Transform Library Space

How:

We will use an ethnographic method known as a "cultural probe." Volunteers from the MIT community will be asked to record their own research behavior over the course of a one-week period using their own digital camera and taking notes in any format they wish. The photos and notes will be used to help each person tell their story in detail during in-depth interviews (1.5 hours).

Who:
Undergrads: Since we know that undergrads are focused mainly on completing coursework, we will study them within the context of specific classes that agree to participate. We aim to target 3 different classes, one from each of the following communities: Science & Engineering, Arts & Humanities, Social Sciences & Management.

For example we may recruit:
- a class working with geospatial data
- a class from comparative media studies using multimedia in some way
- the terrascope class from EAPS, since students work on creating museum-like displays to communicate their content
- a group working from abroad or in an international program (if possible).

We will work with librarian subject liaisons who have existing relationships with specific classes. They will help recruit the particular classes and participate along with UX group members to conduct the interviews.

Grad students, faculty, researchers: Since this group is focused mainly on research, we will study them within the context of specific research projects. We will focus not only on how they find information, but also on how they use, share, and publish it. We aim to target 3 different research projects, again from each of the three communities mentioned above.

We will work with librarian subject liaisons who have existing relationships with specific faculty members. They will help recruit the particular projects to be studied and participate along with UX group members to conduct the interviews.

Library staff involved:
From UX group: Nicole Hennig, Lisa Horowitz, Stephanie Hartman, Remlee Green
from LDLC: Kate McNeill, Michelle Baildon, Anne Graham

How many:
We will have 3 undergrad classes and 3 faculty/grad/researcher projects each with several people willing to participate. We will include undergrad students, teaching assistants, grad students, faculty and researchers. Ideally we'd like to interview 3 people from each class and 2 people from each research project for a total of 15 interviews.

We'll aim to use 4 members of the UX group and 4 subject liaisons from LDLC (TBD). This team of 8 staff will work in pairs to conduct the interviews. (each team of 2 will interview 3-4 people)

The volunteers will be offered $75 Amazon or TechCash gift certificates for their time.

When:
Recruiting & contacting volunteers: throughout February and early March
Participants track themselves: any one week in March or April
Interviews: April/May
Results consolidation: May (first 2 weeks)
Reporting out: May (last 2 weeks)

What:

Interviews will be guided by the following questions:

Warm-up questions:

- Introduce yourselves, explain the process

- Demographic (i.e., who they are and what class or project they did for the study)

The central question:

- So tell us the story of your week. We'll use your diary to jog your memory. Describe any tasks you did during the study that were related to:
finding information, organizing, sharing, citing, collaborating, teaching, presenting, or publishing.

For each task:

Formats:
- What kinds of data and formats did you use? (NOTE: only mention examples if they don't know what you mean)
(i.e., GIS, bioinformatics, social science data sets, textual data, music recordings, images, videos, ebooks, ejournals)

- Describe any difficulties you had with specific formats.

Equipment:
- What kinds of equipment did you use? (NOTE: only mention examples if they don't know what you mean)
(i.e., laptops, mobile phones, smartphones, tablets, desktop computers, cameras, GPS devices, other)

- Describe any difficulties you had with specific equipment.

Collaboration:
- Did you work as an individual, in a group, or both? Tell us about what you do individually vs. what you do in group settings.

- Did you collaborate with remote colleagues? What are some pain points when it comes to collaborating remotely? What works well?

- What were some typical or common pain points in your process?

Change compared to the past:
- How did you do that task differently five years ago? What has become easier and what is still difficult?

- Describe some things that could make this task easier.

Specific tools used:
- How do you save your information, both for the short-term and the longer-term? What happens to your information when the class or research project is over?

- Did you use any academic social research tools, or any general social social tools (in relation to your academic work)?
(i.e., academic: such as Mendeley, Cognet, Archnet, ArXiv, Lablife, Zotero; general social: Facebook or Twitter)

Where & when:
- Where did you do your work? Tell us the specifics of each place that you worked in.
(i.e., an on-campus office, dorm room, coffee shop, library, home or traveling (list city, state, country), plane, train, other.)

- What were some particular qualities of those places that made your work easy or made your work difficult?

- What time of day did you do this work? Are there particular times of day that you prefer for different activities?
(i.e. studying, meetings, research, solitude, thinking, writing, group work)

Getting help:
- Did you ask for or receive help from anyone during the process? Who? What do you consider when deciding whether and who to ask for help?

Publishing:

- What kinds of considerations about copyright, fair use, or open access impacted your work during this time?

- If you have published something recently, tell us about your process. What were the pain points? What would make the process easier for you?

Wrap-up questions:

- (If they haven't mentioned library use yet): Did you use any library services? If so, which ones? How did you find out about them?

- How is your studying or research changing because of new technologies?

- What are the top few things that would make your academic work easier?

Results:

- Each interview will be conducted by a team of two MIT libraries staff. One to conduct the interview and the other to take notes. The UX group will train the library staff participants in ethnographic interviewing techniques.

The notes will be consolidated and a few UX team members will apply card-sorting methods to organizing the results. We'll produce a report and a presentation for MIT Libraries staff. Results will be posted on the UX wiki where all library staff can access them.

The personal identities of MIT community members will not be revealed except to those conducting the interviews. The raw materials (notes and photos) will be stored on a protected wiki space, available only to relevant staff. As we've done in the past, we'll get the study approved by COUHES: http://web.mit.edu/committees/couhes/, and the MIT Libraries staff participating in the study will complete the human subjects training (http://web.mit.edu/committees/couhes/humansubjects.shtml).

ASK A LIBRARIAN   HOURS   OFF-CAMPUS ACCESS   FAQ   CONTACT

Try our new search tool...

more for Friday, May 27

Find Materials   Libraries & Collections   Research & Instruction   Services   News & Events   About

Home » About » Library Feedback

ABOUT

Hours and Locations
Library Feedback
   Overview
   General Feedback
   Feedback About NUcat
   Purchase Suggestion
   Library's New Search Tool - Feedback
Library Administration
Visit the Library
Give to the Library

POPULAR LINKS

→ Library Guides
→ Book Location Guide
→ Apply for Library Jobs
→ Staff Directory

Library Feedback

The Library welcomes feedback regarding its services, resources, and buildings.

We value your suggestions and comments. The library's feedback service is intended for use by current Northwestern students, faculty and staff only. All the information you provide will remain confidential.

General Feedback
General suggestions and feedback to the library on its services, collections and resources

Feedback about NUcat
General feedback about the library's online catalog

Purchase Suggestion
Make a purchase suggestion to a *subject specialist* for a book, journal or electronic resource

Electronic Resources
General feedback about the library's other electronic resources

Gifts
Donate books or other gifts to the library

CONTACT   DISCLAIMER   POLICY STATEMENTS   NU CAMPUS EMERGENCY INFORMATION

Library Home | Northwestern Calendar: PlanIt Purple | Northwestern Search

Northwestern University Library   1970 Campus Drive   Evanston, IL 60208-2300   Evanston: 847.491.7658   Fax: 847.491.8306   library@northwestern.edu

NORTHWESTERN
UNIVERSITY

Establishing fondren@brc

Insights from a User Study

Debra Kolah and Lisa Spiro
August 2010

I. Introduction

Rice University's Bioscience Research Center (BRC) aims to be "a catalyst for new and better ways for researchers to collaborate, explore, learn and lead."[1] With fondren@brc, its new library facility in the BRC, Fondren Library can participate in this collaborative effort and support researchers in producing pioneering new research. Through fondren@brc, the library can explore how to use a flexible library space that focuses on service instead of content, what kind of services to offer to a group of scientists who mainly do their research online, and how to implement embedded librarianship, or the integration of librarians into academic disciplines.

To understand how best to serve the biochemists, bioengineers, and chemists who occupy the BRC, Debra Kolah and Lisa Spiro interviewed 3 faculty members, 4 graduate students, and a library liaison (to date; more interviews are planned). We adopted the ethnographic research methods developed by anthropologist Nancy Foster through her work at the University of Rochester, methods that we learned by attending a workshop Foster taught for the Council on Library and Information Resources (CLIR). We conducted half-hour to hour long semi-structured interviews, examining how researchers do their work, how they use the BRC, and what services they would like to see the library offer.

II. How Bioscience Researchers Use the Library

Bioscience researchers primarily work in their labs, so they want easy online access to the research literature. Occasionally, they will walk to the library, but more frequently it is a graduate student who is tasked with picking up materials at Fondren Library. One researcher commented on missing the new book shelf, but it is Fondren is too far to go by now.

Researchers primarily use Web of Science, Scopus, and Pubmed. Even though researchers may say "I don't really use the library," they often proceed to acknowledge that they use multiple online databases. There remains a gap in the perception that it is the library that is providing the subscriptions to the research database.

---

[1]http://www.rice.edu/brc/index.shtml

Interlibrary loan seems to be the most heavily used service, and researchers seem very happy with all aspects of it. Course reserves do not seem to be used by the faculty we interviewed. Instead, professors seem to be putting their own resources into their courses on OwlSpace.

The subject bibliographer has witnessed a steady decline in the number of office visits over the past five years, and now "face to face contact has diminished to the point where I hardly ever see them." Faculty still do email requests and questions, but some faculty seem not read all email sent to them, so communication remains challenging. However, the department liaisons work closely with the subject bibliographers.

The faculty we interviewed knew very little about the fondren@brc space and were confused by the sign by the door describing it as "TMC Library." One faculty member seemed to get somewhat upset after hearing that the library would not provide access to Med Center information resources. Fondren needs to communicate its mission and services for the BRC space clearly.

III. Life at the BRC

Located at 6500 Main Street, the BRC links Rice with the Medical Center. Currently the BRC hosts faculty, postdocs, graduate students, undergraduate researchers, and affiliated staff in bioengineering (which is wholly located in the BRC), biochemistry, and chemistry. Currently 27 Rice faculty and their research groups are located in the BRC. In addition, the offices for Gulf Coast Consortia (GCC) and the Cancer Prevention and Research Institute of Texas (CPRIT) are based at the BRC. The ten-story building features several lounges, conference rooms, a 28-seat auditorium, a 90 seat seminar room, "state-of-the-art classrooms," and 10,000 square feet of retail space (which is as of yet unoccupied). To connect the BRC to the main Rice campus, a Rice shuttle service stops at the BRC four times an hour and delivers passengers to campus in less than 10 minutes. A pleasant walking path links the BRC and central campus.

Most faculty spend the majority of their time at the BRC, although occasionally they go to the central campus to attend lectures or meetings, teach classes, or interact with seminar speakers. Some classes are held in the BRC, mostly in bioengineering. Graduate students tend to spend more time on campus, but seem to regard the distance between the central campus and the BRC as being significant, so they prefer to drive rather than walk. Most of what researchers need is available at the BRC, although they would like a cafe (one is being planned).

When researchers moved into the BRC in the fall of 2009, the physical infrastructure was not completely in place. Initially administrators at the BRC focused on the physical structure of the building, resolving issues such as plumbing problems. Now, work is being done to build the "social fabric" of the BRC by promoting both "vertical" and "horizontal" integration within the building, so that researchers know their neighbors on their own floors and throughout the building. The BRC deliberately mixes together researchers from different departments on the same floor. To promote community, the BRC hosts a Tuesday morning Bagels and Brew, in which different campus and vendor groups come in to showcase their products and services; a recent Bagels and Brew focused on biosafety and compliance issues. The events aim both to foster community and to disseminate information so that people can accomplish their goals more easily. The BRC also hosts a Thursday afternoon event called Patties on the Patio. Signs promoting these events adorn the elevators and other public spaces. The hallways are lined with posters showcasing research going on at the BRC, and some researchers have drawn or written on the glass walls.

Fondren's space in the BRC is located on the second floor, just beyond an entranceway that is linked to the patio by a spiral staircase. It seems that Fondren's facility is in a fairly visible, high traffic area, although our observation of the space occurred during the summer, when most students are away and when construction was altering foot traffic through the building,

IV. Recommendations/Conclusion

We concluded our interviews by asking for suggestions for Fondren's BRC facility. Interviewees suggested that the library provide the following:

Services
1. Most of all, researchers wanted access to **biomedical databases** that are available at the HAM-TMC library. They didn't understand why they cannot access these important research materials. One interviewee suggested that it might be possible to offer faculty joint appointments with Medical Center institutions so that they could access these databases; Rice could give Med Center faculty reciprocal privileges. Such an approach worked (to some extent) at another institution.
2. **Pick up and drop off services** for books that researchers needed to acquire or return. Although researchers don't use print books very frequently, occasionally they want to consult an introductory book, specialty work, or older volume. Making the trip to Fondren can be cumbersome. As one interviewee commented, "it doesn't seem like 15 minutes is much to walk, but it is."
3. **Training and support for patent searches**.
4. **Training and support for the development of business plans**.
5. Although fondren@brc does not need to be open for extensive hours, librarians can offer **regular office hours** so that researchers can drop by with questions. Not only would researchers better know their librarian, but librarians would develop a deeper understanding of the researcher community that they are serving. Graduate students in particular said that they would like to get help identifying and accessing relevant resources.
6. Host **outreach sessions** focused on "what the library can do for you." Perhaps the library can host a future Bagels and Brew or Patties on the Patio event. As one interviewee told us, "Feed them and they will come." The best times for such events seem to be weekday mornings (10 a.m.) and afternoons (4 p.m.).
7. Offer **tutorials and workshops**. A number of researchers (particularly graduate

students) come from other countries and may not be familiar with library resources or how to find what they need. Workshops would be especially useful for first-year graduate students who may not be familiar with doing serious library research. Faculty seemed supportive of new graduate students attending workshops focused on their research areas, and graduate students seemed interested in such workshops as well. Short workshops that teach researchers how to do their work more quickly and efficiently might also be popular. In addition, researchers need specialized training in working with Web Of Science, medical databases, tech transfer, patents, business, and environmental science.

8. **Survey** BRC tenant groups about what they need, particularly when it comes to journals and other information resources.
9. Raise awareness of library services by sending a **BRC specific email**.

Facilities and Collections

10. **Space that can be used for meetings**. Already at least one small conference session has been held in the current Fondren space.
11. **Access to high-end printing**, particularly poster printing. Typically each lab will produce about 10 posters per year, according to one interviewee.
12. **Access to high-end computer workstations**, particularly with expensive software such as SAS, MatLab, Adobe products, Mathematica, etc. Large displays would also be helpful. Graduate students particularly identified this as a need.
13. **A small collection of new books**. One researcher commented that it was difficult to know "if there's anything new at the library," but that a display of these books would be useful. Alternatively, perhaps the subject specialist could compile a quarterly update of new books relevant to a discipline and circulate that via email.
14. A comfortable, flexible space for **collaborative student projects**.
15. **Video conferencing** for meetings with other research groups. (It appears that some video conferencing facilities are already in the BRC.)
16. A **small journal browsing collection**. Each research group could provide a list of 5-10 core publications that they would like to see in the building.
17. A **touchscreen display** showing you what is available in the library.

In addition to the researchers' suggestions, we recommend that:

1. The library embrace the visual culture of the BRC and **promote library services** and resources through posters facing the hallway, colorful drawings on the glass walls, flyers in the elevators, and other marketing approaches.
2. Fondren sponsor **outreach sessions**. The hallway outside the library space in the BRC is large enough to accommodate several tables as well as groups of people, so food could be served there.
3. Librarians create a BRC **Libguide** that reflects the interdisciplinary research needs of the building and provides links to resources in biology, chemistry, bioengineering, and biophysics.
4. More marketing and training can be done for **Scopus**, which is generally a better citation

database for emerging sciences such as bioengineering.
5. Innovative technologies that foster communication between the library@brc and Fondren be explored: use of **Skype** and **GoogleChat**, for example.

Faculty and graduate students whom we interviewed seemed to have a generally positive impression of the library and to welcome help in getting access to information that they need. With the fondren@brc space, Fondren has the opportunity to explore new models of librarianship based not so much on collections as on services.

SUMMARY

NEW BRUNSWICK STUDENT FOCUS GROUPS, SPRING 2008

The Rutgers University Libraries held three student focus groups in New Brunswick during spring semester 2008. The impetus for having these groups was the desire of the current Reference and Lobby Redesign Committee to know from students what kinds of spaces they wanted in the library. There was also a desire to know from students their perceptions and desires of reference service. In addition, the libraries have been seeking information from graduate students about a possible redesign of the Graduate Reading Room. To this end we held three focus groups: March 26 for undergraduates (two students) and one for graduate students (5 students); and April 23 for undergraduates. (eight students). Lila Fredenburg facilitated the discussions; and Jeanne Boyle, Valeda Dent, and Françoise Puniello took notes.

The following questions directed the discussions:

1. We often hear that atmosphere is important for studying. What do you think is the ideal atmosphere for individual study? Group Study?

2. What three things do you like most about the library? What three things do you like the least about it?

3. What do you imagine being in the perfect university library?

4. What do you imagine the perfect graduate reading room looking like? What do you imagine the perfect undergraduate study space?

5. What do you think is meant by reference service?

6. Do the services offered by the library meet your needs?

7. What would make reference service better?

SUMMARY OF THEMES

1. Overall - All Groups

Appropriate study spaces - quiet and group

Hours – especially weekends and late night

Complexity of library website

Outlets for laptop use

2. Undergraduate Students

Quiet spaces

Hours

Computing - wireless, access to computers

Aesthetics

More seats

3. Graduate Students

Comfortable and diverse spaces

Equipment and costs to use

Digital resources and services

Librarian contact and help

FSP/JEB 5/20/08

RUTGERS
University Libraries

STAFF RESOURCES

| BOOKROOM | FIND PEOPLE | FIND COMMITTEES | SEARCH STAFF PAGES | STAFF RESOURCES INDEX |

- Libraries Home
- Staff Resources Home
- Access Services
- Administrative Services
- Budget Office
- Central Technical Services
- Collection Development
- Distributed Technical Services
- Human Resources
- Integrated Information Systems
- Library Faculty
- Marketing
- Planning and Assessment
- Public Services
- Research and Instructional Services
- Technical and Automated Services
- Training & Development
- University Librarian

- Sampling Dates
- Abbreviations & Acronyms

Rutgers University Libraries Staff Resources:
Planning and Assessment:
Committees and Task Forces:

Ethnographic Research Project: Reports

Studying Students: The Ethnographic Research Project at Rutgers

- Studying Students to Enhance Library Services at Rutgers University: Principles and Priorities for Moving from Research to Redesign and Development of the Libraries Website: The Final Report of Our Ethnographic Research Project [PDF]

- Tentative Findings from Student Surveys and Interviews as Compiled at the Conclusion of the Research Phase of the Rutgers University Libraries Web Interface Redesign Project [PDF]

- Qualitative Findings from Student Interviews as Compiled at the Conclusion of the Research Phase of the Rutgers University Libraries Web Interface Redesign Project [PDF]

Coded Comments

- Graduate Students [Excel]
- Undergraduate Students [Excel]

Comment Reports from Committees and Other Groups

- Alumni [PDF]
- Ask a Librarian [PDF]
- Circulation [PDF]
- Citation Managers [PDF]
- Collections [PDF]
- Communicate [PDF]
- Facilities [PDF]
- Federated Searching, Vendor Issues [PDF]
- Hours, Maps, Navigation, Research Guides, Visuals [PDF]
- Instruction [PDF]
- Interlibrary Loan [PDF]
- IRIS [PDF]
- Navigation [PDF]
- Personalization [PDF]
- Proxy [PDF]
- Research Guides [PDF]

- Comments Distribution Message [PDF]
- Comments Distribution Table [PDF]

State of the Libraries 2009 Presentation PowerPoint Slides [PDF]

Last updated September 28, 2009; December 9, 2009; February 15, 2010; March 24, 2010

RUTGERS
University Libraries

STUDYING STUDENTS TO ENHANCE LIBRARY SERVICES AT RUTGERS UNIVERSITY:

PRINCIPLES AND PRIORITIES FOR MOVING FROM RESEARCH TO REDESIGN AND DEVELOPMENT OF THE LIBRARIES WEBSITE

THE FINAL REPORT OF OUR ETHNOGRAPHIC RESEARCH PROJECT

Submitted by:

Grace Agnew
Ka-Neng Au
Susan J. Beck
Jeanne Boyle
Judith Gardner
Samuel McDonald
Rhonda Marker
Chad Mills

March 17, 2010

STUDYING STUDENTS TO ENHANCE LIBRARY SERVICES AT RUTGERS UNIVERSITY:

PRINCIPLES AND PRIORITIES FOR MOVING FROM RESEARCH TO REDESIGN AND DEVELOPMENT OF THE LIBRARIES WEBSITE

THE FINAL REPORT OF OUR ETHNOGRAPHIC RESEARCH PROJECT

INTRODUCTION

We carried out this ethnographic research project to investigate the research behaviors of Rutgers University undergraduate students, graduate students, and faculty in an effort to discover how library and information resources are used, in particular the Rutgers University Libraries website. We intended that the research would highlight ways in which the website might be improved both to enhance the research experience for users and to attract new users.

This final report details the principles and priorities developed by the core team for guiding improvements to the Libraries website. Project methods and detailed results are contained in two reports available on the Libraries website at: http://www.libraries.rutgers.edu/rul/staff/groups/ethnography/reports.shtml. Also at the same location are coded comments from the surveys of graduate and undergraduate students and review reports with specific recommendations from relevant councils and committees on the coded comments contributed by survey respondents.

The study gathered a great deal of data. The various reports describe the "what" of improving our website. The design team will determine the "how."

PRIMARY FINDING

The Libraries website needs to be viewed quite differently by librarians and library staff than it has been to date. Instead of being a vehicle for library information, it must become a tool. Website users do not want to read and be instructed, except perhaps by choice. They desperately need and want the website to carry out actively what they need to have done. As Roy Tennant has written:

> "You know you want it. Or you know someone who does. One search box and a button to search a variety of sources, with results collated for easy review. Go ahead, give in—after all, isn't it true that only librarians like to search? Everyone else likes to *find*."[1]

Our results confirm this view.

---

[1] Digital Libraries- Cross-Database Search: One-Stop Shopping, by Roy Tennant. Library Journal, 10/15/01. Viewed February 3, 2010: http://www.libraryjournal.com/article/CA170458.html.

1

PRINCIPLES

These principles should guide current and future redesign and development of the Libraries website:

1. Flexibility. Users should be able to customize both their experience and where they receive information as individuals and as members of groups.

2. Integration. The Libraries website needs to integrate more tightly with such user tools as Sakai, the university website, myRutgers, departmental websites, continuous education, RUcore.

3. Information literacy. The Libraries website should express and be an integral part of information literacy learning at the university.

4. Simplicity. Less is definitely more. The Libraries website should be easy to get to and remember, with fewer clicks and explicit language.

5. Context. Website users should always know where they are and how they got there.

6. Self-sufficiency. People want to find and do for themselves. Tool development should focus on self-sufficiency.

7. Process. There needs to be an iterative and permanent process of redesign and development that incorporates version releases, constant rethinking of strategy, and constant feedback.

PRIORITIES

After reviewing all reports and comments, the Core Team has identified the following priorities for initial website redesign and development. They are listed by priority within broad categories. The categories themselves are not prioritized but are listed alphabetically.

Access
Single sign-on/login – Users desire one login for all services we offer. It should be integrated with the login for remote access. They report not being able to access resources remotely without paying.
E-Journal process
E-journal process – Our process for finding e-journals and articles in them is undeniably broken. Users need improved discovery, navigation, URL access, selection by discipline, and enhanced federated searching capabilities. They come to us needing a particular article or wanting articles on a particular topic, and we present them with lists of database and journal titles. They scroll over Searchlight and do not see that it might be the single search box they desire. Users search our databases or Google Scholar and cannot figure out how to link to our e-articles even when we offer them. Users experience requests for payment when accessing our resources remotely.
Help users identify databases to use for their research – The broad subject breakdowns of indexes and databases, advanced search subject choices within Searchlight, and the research guides are not doing the job. They need to be brought together and surfaced.

2

RUTGERS UNIVERSITY

Studying Students to Enhance Library Services at Rutgers University
http://www.libraries.rutgers.edu/rul/staff/groups/ethnography/reports/ERP_Final_Report.pdf

Navigation

Navigation – Users want to find rather than search and search rather than read instructions.

Surface high demand resources – We need to aggressively and continually identify our high demand resources and give them top real estate. Titles mentioned often are Academic Search Premier and JSTOR; one Web page in demand is our Hours and Directions. What are the others? How do we feature them?

Match user expectation in Web 2.0 in color layout, widgets, and services – This is not currently among our first priorities.

Search – Many users desire one Google-like search box. We need to improve our federated search function, extending it to more databases and to such other tools as our website, IRIS, RUcore, etc.

Personalization and context – point of need

Personalization features – Users want to manage their favorite resources.

Delivery of services to tools outside the Libraries context – Several users requested the availability of maps that would guide to a particular book in our stacks. Such maps could be on a cell phone as the user walks to the stacks. Other places to deliver our services include departmental websites, Sakai, myRutgers, etc.

Create different Web spaces for different user groups - Users come to us with different levels of expectation and skills as well as different needs dependent on discipline and status.

Help when needed – Users requested such helps as one-minute podcasts at point of need and very brief text when they stumble.

Research guides - Users don't want to bother librarians. We need to explore making on demand/online librarians more available and investigate how to incorporate provision of subject expertise in a discipline.

Simplifying

Change labels – While we constantly strive to minimize library jargon, our users want us to do better and give them an easier to use website.

Repave – We need to get rid of tripping spots, extra clicks, etc.

Top page

Service orientation on top page – The website should provide services supported by lower pages rather than lists of resources.

Front page delivery – The left hand menu is too cute, crowded, etc.

STRATEGIES

Suggested strategies for managing the web redesign and development are:

1. Unify redesign, development, and ongoing oversight of the website by integrating the responsibilities and functions of the Web Advisory Committee (WAC) and Web Services into one new group. Include representation from the IRIS Public Access Committee (IPAC). Recognize that the silos of website content, technology, and public catalog are a library construct and are not meaningful to users, who rightly integrate the services in their mind.

3

2. Work with other groups, as appropriate, such as the Digital Interface Group (DIG), for implementing changes to the e-journal process. Leverage existing expertise and service/resource management processes to add efficiency, integration, and different points of view and expertise to the redesign and development process.

3. Recognize that website redesign and development is an ongoing process that needs to reflect changing user needs and changing technologies and not a discrete and massive project occurring every 3-5 years. Develop a version schedule for incremental, ongoing changes. Schedule at least two website versions annually.

4. Identify and prioritize website functionalities into coherent and coordinated website version releases.

5. Recognize dependencies/interrelationship to other developments, such as the selection of a new open source public access catalog for VALE that would be a strong candidate for the new public catalog interface for RUL. Other dependencies include integration with services offered via OIT (Sakai, myRutgers, etc.), changes to RUcore, etc.

OTHER ISSUES

Several remaining issues point to possible future activities:

1. At the request of the Core Team, Jeanne Boyle, the remaining principal investigator for this project, filed a successful request for continuing review with the Institutional Research Board to give us flexibility in following up with users for clarification, feedback, etc. The Core Team remains ready to oversee any additional data gathering required. We encourage all library faculty and staff to consult existing ethnographic data or use Google Analytics or RUL website statistics before beginning new data gathering projects.

2. We need to market the website redesign and development process more actively within the Libraries.

3. The website redesign and development process needs to be informed by the differences between user and librarian beliefs, which in itself is one of the key take-aways from the ERP study.

4. Research guides and other current similar efforts need to have their assumptions challenged not only for service effectiveness but also for return on investment. Students are asking to be directed to the appropriate resources particular to their specific research needs. Research guides have traditionally been the Libraries approach to addressing this need, but students don't seem to be generally aware of research guides. Are the libraries receiving a useful return on investment for research guides, given the amount of time and effort involved in creating a research guide? Should more agile and dynamic approaches, such as packaging resources into custom portals, be employed instead? What are our peer institutions doing? It was agreed that the evaluation of the research guide methodology is out of scope for this working group but that the research guide strategy should be evaluated, in light of ERP findings, perhaps by a specific working group tasked by the two councils.

5. Additional recommendations for website improvement are included in the review reports from relevant councils and committees on the Libraries website.

4

NEXT STEPS

Judy Gardner, Interim Deputy Associate University Librarian for Research and Instructional Services, has been charged to coordinate improvements to our Web presence and digital public services, including work resulting from the ethnographic study and the need to advance implementation of its recommendations. She will partner with the Director of Integrated Information Systems for the Rutgers University Libraries to guarantee that the appropriate commitment and support from both public services and information technology are brought to bear on developing the Libraries website. Judy and the Director will work with members of the newly integrated website team and the Core Team to initiate and oversee the redesign and development process.

Information gathered in this study concerns issues beyond just the Libraries website. All committees and other groups that reviewed comments from the student survey will be requested to review their initial recommendations, taking into consideration the principles, priorities, and strategies in this report, which focuses on the website, as well as the website-focused and more general recommendations in the report on student interviews. They will be requested to incorporate work that will carry out both the website and other recommendations into their planning and goal setting for academic year 2011 and beyond. The Core Team will provide support in the form of additional data gathering and analysis and priority setting, as needed, and track and report on progress over the course of the coming academic year.

5

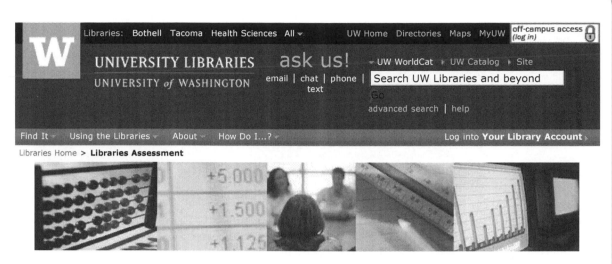

UW Libraries Assessment

Libraries Assessment & Metrics Team

Members
Presentations
Publications

Charge

The Libraries Assessment and Metrics Team works with and reports to the Director of Assessment and Planning to:

* initiate and support library assessment efforts within the University Libraries;
* identify user needs and assess Libraries efforts at meeting them;
* foster a culture of assessment within the Libraries;
* provide support as needed for assessment efforts conducted by other library staff;
* develop expertise and understanding of assessment measures and techniques and share these with library staff as needed;
* conduct the Libraries triennial user surveys;
* communicate assessment activities and results to appropriate individuals and groups;
* assist in assessing organizational performance through the development of outcomes and success metrics;
* help develop a management information infrastructure to make data and key statistics available to staff and the public;
* maintain the library assessment Web sites;
* and plan the semiannual library assessment forums.

Contact Us
Last modified: Thursday January 27, 2011

UW Libraries Triennial Survey

The University of Washington Libraries has conducted extensive large-scale surveys of faculty and students since 1992. These triennial surveys focus on library use and satisfaction as well as user needs and library priorities.

2010 Triennial Survey Forms & Results NEW! *Updated 12 November 2010

Previous Triennial Surveys and Results

Other Surveys, Results & Assessment Info

In Library Use Surveys
Reports
Usability Testing

Library Statistics

KEY FACTS - University Libraries: Contribution to UW Excellence (PDF) *Updated 10/09
Selected Library Statistics
User Query Sampling
Circulation Statistics
Monthly Gate Counts (.xls)

Libraries Home > Libraries Assessment > Surveys > Ilu2005 > **In Library Use Surveys**

In Library Use Surveys

Forms and Results

2008

Survey Forms	Results
	Frequency Tables (.doc) Datasheets (.xls)
Branch Library Form (.doc) UW Bothell Library Form (.doc) UW Tacoma Library Form (.doc) Health Sciences Library Form (.doc) Odegaard Undergraduate Library Form (.doc) Suzzallo-Allen Libraries Form (.doc)	**CHARTS** NEW! (Click here for instructions on how to create custom charts.) Question 1: What did you do in this library today? Question 3: How important are the services? Question 4: How would you rate the library? Question 5: Who are you? *(respondent status)*

2005

Survey Forms	Results
	Frequency Tables (.doc) Datasheets (.xls)
Branch Library Form (.doc) Health Sciences Library Form (.doc) Odegaard Undergraduate Library Form (.doc) Suzzallo-Allen Libraries Form (.doc)	**CHARTS** (Click here for instructions on how to create custom charts.) Question 1: What did you do in this library today? Question 3: How important are the services? Question 4: How would you rate the library? Question 5: Who are you? *(respondent status)*

2002

Survey Forms	Results
Branch Library Form (.doc) Odegaard Undergraduate Library Form (.doc) Suzzallo-Allen Libraries Form (.doc)	Frequency Tables (.doc)

Contact Us
Last modified: Monday March 30, 2009

Libraries Home ┊ Site Map ┊ Site Search ┊ Contact Us

© 1998-2011 University of Washington Libraries
Box 352900 Seattle, WA 98195-2900 USA
phone: 206-543-0242

IN-LIBRARY USE SURVEY 2008	BRANCH LIBRARY	Date _____	Survey No._____

Please take a few minutes to complete this survey **BEFORE** you leave and help us evaluate library services.
Drop the survey off in any of the boxes marked "library survey" near the exit. Thank you.

1. What did you do in this library today? (Please check all that apply)

a.___ Asked library staff for assistance

b.___ Looked for books, journals or other items in the library

c.___ Used course reserves

d.___ Borrowed or returned material

e.___ Made photocopies

f.___ LOCAL QUESTION

g.___ LOCAL QUESTION

h.___ Studied individually or did own work

i.___ Studied or worked in a group

j.___ Used a library computer

k.___ Used personal laptop or mobile computing device

l.___ Met friends/someone else

m.___ Printed from computer

n.___ Other (please specify)

2. How often do you visit this library in person? (Please check the most appropriate category)

❏4 or more times per week   ❏2-3 times per week   ❏Weekly   ❏Monthly   ❏Less often   ❏This is my first time here

3. How important are the following services to you in this library? (If service isn't currently available here mark how important it would be to offer it in this library)

	Very Important				Not important
Library computers	5	4	3	2	1
Assistance from library staff	5	4	3	2	1
Access to on-site collections	5	4	3	2	1
Access to online library resources	5	4	3	2	1
Place to work individually	5	4	3	2	1
Place to work in groups	5	4	3	2	1
Application software on library computers (Word, Excel)	5	4	3	2	1
Electrical outlets by seating areas	5	4	3	2	1
LOCAL QUESTION	5	4	3	2	1
LOCAL QUESTION	5	4	3	2	1

4. How would you rate this library on the following?

	Excellent			Poor		Not applicable
Access to computers	5	4	3	2	1	0
Space where I can work on my own	5	4	3	2	1	0
Space where I can work with groups	5	4	3	2	1	0
Quality of collections	5	4	3	2	1	0
Quality of customer service	5	4	3	2	1	0
Ease of finding collection locations and service points	5	4	3	2	1	0
Hours open	5	4	3	2	1	0
Inviting environment	5	4	3	2	1	0
LOCAL QUESTION	5	4	3	2	1	0

5. Who are you? (Check one category that best applies to your visit today)

___UW undergraduate student
   Declared Major_____

___Student at other college
___K-12 student

___UW graduate/professional student
   Department_____

___Instructor or staff at other school
___Businessperson/professional

___UW faculty or staff
   Department_____

___Community member/public
___Other (please specify)

6. Briefly list what we can do to make this library better for you. Include any other comments here or on back.

UNIVERSITY OF WATERLOO

Porter Main Floor Renovation. Furniture Charrette – Summary of Results

Porter Main Floor Renovation

Furniture Charrette - Summary of Results

January 15, 2008

9 students participated. Students were asked to provide furniture layout input into three areas but were welcome to comment on any part of the floor. The three areas are: Southwest corner (SW); Southeast corner (SE); Browsers seating area (BR).

Southwest

- 2 recommended the area be devoted to **group** table space (mixture of booths, pods, small and large tables)
- 1 recommended a mixture of **group** tables (booth) and **workstations** (line)
- 1 recommended a mixture of **group** tables (booths and large tables), **workstations** (line), and **laptop** counter in the corner
- 1 recommended a mixture of group table (booths and large table) and **comfy** sofas with coffee tables
- 1 recommended a mixture of small **group** tables, **comfy** group in the middle of tables and laptop, and **laptop** at front window
- 1 recommended of mixture of comfy **group**, comfy **individual**, and **workstation** (line) in the middle of area
- 1 recommended almost entirely **workstation** (line – as many as possible) with some **laptop** at side window
- 1 recommended entirely **café** seating

Comments on this area: "Group/collaboration area (workstation pods but without workstations). These tables are good as each member of a group has plenty of their own desk space but can see each other and talk to each other (not as silent as upstairs)"
Summary – mostly table group (booths and tables), some workstations, some comfy group and a little comfy individual

Southeast

- 1 recommended all **laptop** in two lines parallel to front window
- 1 recommended mostly **laptop** with some **workstation** (laptop in same two lines as above, but with workstation (line) in the middle if room
- 1 recommended mostly **laptop** (front window and aisle) with one large **group** table and one **café** seating
- 1 recommended mostly **laptop** (along both windows) with three **café** seating

- 1 recommended **mixed comfy** – some couches some chairs
- 1 recommended mixture of **laptop** against Graphics parallel to workstation, and **workstation** (line) along front window
- 1 recommended an even mixture of **café** along both windows and two **laptop** counters
- 1 recommended a **laptop** counter along front window and four small **group** tables
- 1 recommended entirely **laptop** along side window and along aisle by stairs

Comments on this area: "Most students don't know about this space. Once they see others working on laptops, from the large windows, they can also begin to use it"
Summary – mostly laptop, some café and a little workstation

Browsers

- 1 recommended **laptop**, **café** only by window, 2 **group** collaboration booths and mixed style of **workstation**
- 1 recommended two **workstation** pods and three **individual tables** by window
- 1 recommended lots of **café** seating, occasional table, two **sofas** and two **comfy chair**s
- 1 recommended two **workstation** pods, a **laptop** counter by window, interspersed with **individual table** study
- 1 recommended lots of **café** and some **individual and group comfy** seating with coffee table by window
- 1 recommended all **workstation**
- 1 recommended three **café** style and six **comfy sofas** by the window with coffee tables in between every two
- 1 recommended two **café** style interspersed with two **comfy chairs** (wants area to stay the same)
- 1 recommended one **café** style, three individual **comfy chairs**, one **sofa** and two occasional tables all by the window

Comments on this area: "The café/comfy area is a nice place to grab a coffee and read the newspaper or that interesting book you picked up. When one person has grabbed a table, no one else will sit there and several chairs are wasted. Let's give the option for the individuals to sit on comfy chairs while there is café space available for when you run into your friend"
"I think that café style seating should stay the same"
Summary - two camps: one is comfy cafe and one is workstations and laptops i.e. individual work activity

Additional Comments: "There is plenty of space from floors 6-10 for individual, secluded study. The main floor, especially with the large windows, would be a better area for groups to meet and collaborate. (Especially as your friends can spot you from outside"

"One thing I normally do is bring my laptop to work at an individual table upstairs. A laptop bench to plug in properly would be a welcome change"

"Perhaps make the laptop benches less elongated. It may be a little intimidating to see a long row of benches. I think this layout [referring to the "mushroom" pods] for laptop space would be preferable as it gives people plenty of personal space while being efficient with the room size"
"The first floor of the DP should be as informal as possible. There are lots of other floors that are more formal study areas"

"I also think that the furniture should be as movable as possible so students can move the furniture to suit their needs"

"Individual siting [sic] with sofas (group discussion)" in the area marked INDIVIDUAL STUDY

"Laptop 'lockdown feature'" on laptop counters

Print release stations in alcove beside information desk and in public work area

Informal Interview

Questions

1. What do you come into the library for?

2. Is there anything; a service, equipment, or resource missing in the library?

3. As you enter the library, what would you like to see?

4. What service points do you use?

5. What do you like about the library? & dislike?

Don't just sit there,
Speak your mind...

The library wants your feedback on the best way to use
the main floor at Porter!

Here's how
3. Answer the questions on the other side of this card
4. Drop off your completed card in the box on the table at the exit.

If you have already filled out one of these cards,
please leave this one for the next person

April 2007

What kind of seating is most important for the <u>main floor at Porter?</u>

Please rank the following items, 1 being most important and 6 being the least important.

__group study tables   __individual study tables

__individual study carrels   __group study rooms

__comfy lounge furniture and tables   __more café seating

If group study rooms went onto the <u>main floor at Porter</u>, what additional equipment should they contain?

Please rank the following items, 1 being most important and 5 being the least important.

__computer with large screen for group work   __white board

__large screen but no computer (plug-in your own laptop)   __flip chart paper

__other (please specify) _____

What do you like best about the <u>main floor at Porter?</u> _____

_____

What would you change about the <u>main floor at Porter?</u> _____

_____

Is there anything else you would like us to know? _____

_____

Advisory Boards

The screenshot shows a UBC Irving K. Barber Learning Centre web page.

Navigation bar: Campuses + | UBC Directories + | UBC QuickLinks +

UBC — a place of mind — THE UNIVERSITY OF BRITISH COLUMBIA — IRVING K BARBER LEARNING CENTRE

HOME | ABOUT US | FACILITIES | PROGRAMS AND SERVICES | LIBRARY SERVICES @ IKBLC | SUPPORT US | WEBCASTS

ADVISORY COMMITTEE

Home » About Us

About Us
- » Charter
- » Irving K. Barber
- » Funders and Partners
- » Advisory Committee
- » Community Engagement
- » Feedback
- » Contact Us
- » Newsletter

WHY AN ADVISORY COMMITTEE?

In order to create a wider forum for discussion and consideration of the role and activities of the Learning Centre, we established the IKBLC Advisory Committee. The Advisory Committee's membership includes UBC and community stakeholders to ensure that program advice represents a broad range of interests and perspectives with respect to the IKBLC's expansive mission, with primary focus on the external community-oriented services.

While the Committee is not a Steering Committee, IKBLC staff ask the Committee to engage in a wide range of discussions and make informed recommendations as to Learning Centre service priorities and development, and we, in turn, take Committee recommendations seriously, followuing up on directions and ideas.

(Photo Credit: Glenn Drexhage)

2010-2011 MEMBERS

- Scott Graham, Director of Community Development Education, Social Policy and Research Council of BC (SPARC BC)
- Sue Hanley, Coordinator, First Nations Technology Council
- Cathy Mercer, Director of Student and Enrolment Services, Selkirk College
- Nancy Levesque, University Library Director, Thompson Rivers University
- Rory McIvor, Director, Community Futures Development Corporation of Okanagan Similkameen
- Doug McLachlan, Vice-President, Education, College of the Rockies
- Eve Hope, Head Librarian, Hazelton District Public Library
- Deanna Nyce, President of Wilp Wilxo'oskwhl Nisga'a Institute, located in Gitwinksihlkw
- Chris van der Mark, Superintendent, School District 54, Bulkley Valley
- Andy Ackerman, Trustee, Fort St. John Public Library Board, President, British Columbia Library Trustees Association
- Vacant, Graduate Student Society, UBC
- Ben Cappellacci, VP Academic and University Affairs, Alma Mater Society, UBC
- Ian Cavers, Associate Dean, Curriculum and Learning, Faculty of Science, UBC
- Janet Giltrow, Associate Dean, Students, Faculty of Arts, UBC

- Linc Kesler, Director, First Nations Studies Program and Director & Sr. Advisor to the President on Aboriginal Affairs
- Michelle Lamberson, Managing Director, Centre for Teaching, Learning and Technology, UBC
- Janet Teasdale, Director, Student Development, UBC
- Jan Wallace, Head Librarian, David Lam Management Research Library, UBC
- Chris Petty, Director of Communications, Alumni Association, UBC
- Don Black, Director of Community Programs, Continuing Studies, UBC
- Michelle Aucoin, Managing Director of Community Engagement, External, Legal and Community Relations, UBC
- Cynthia Mathieson, Acting Dean, Irving K. Barber School of Arts and Sciences, UBCO
- Leonora Crema, Associate University Librarian, Planning and Community Relations, UBC

- Ex officio: Ingrid Parent, UBC University Librarian
- Ex officio: Irving K. Barber

a place of mind
THE UNIVERSITY OF BRITISH COLUMBIA

UBC Library

The Irving K. Barber Learning Centre
University of British Columbia
Fax: (604) 822-3242
Contact us

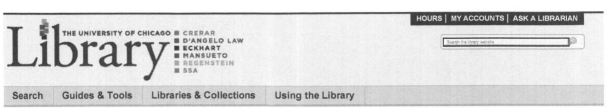

Search | Guides & Tools | Libraries & Collections | Using the Library

Library Home > About the Library > Library Student Resource Group

Library Student Resource Group

The Library Student Resource Group (LSRG) serves as a formal channel of communication between students and the Library Administration. The LSRG discusses matters related to all the University libraries—Crerar, D'Angelo Law, Eckhart, Mansueto, Regenstein, and SSA—including feedback about collections, access, services, and present and future needs of the student community. The LSRG also assists in making specific recommendations to improve the Library and considers proposals for future changes in services. Finally, members of the LSRG discuss how the Library can most effectively communicate its resources, services and plans with students, and conversely, how students can most effectively communicate their wishes, needs and concerns to the Library.

The student representation in the LSRG consists of students from the College, Divisions, and the Professional Schools, who represent their respective areas. The LSRG also includes several Library staff, including the Library Director.

The Council meets approximately 2 times per quarter, with the year's dates selected at the first meeting. Students are appointed to the LSRG by Deans of Students, working with the Office of the Vice President and Dean of Students in the University, and serve a 2-year term.

Membership

From the College, the Divisions, and the Professional Schools:

- Joey Brown, College
- Allison Demes, College
- Samantha Lee, College
- Rachel Miller, College
- Julia Sizek, College
- Nicholas Stock, College

- Mark Opal, Biological Sciences Division
- Joshua Grochow, Physical Sciences Division
- Ben Merriman, Social Sciences Division
- Chris Dunlap, Social Sciences Division
- Rick Moore, Social Sciences Division
- Peter Erickson, Humanities Division
- Nick Tarasen, Law School
- Kelly Ledbetter, Pritzker School of Medicine

From the Library:

- Judith Nadler, Library Director, *chair*
- Jim Vaughan, Assistant Director for Access and Facilities
- Rachel Rosenberg, Communications Director
- John Kimbrough, Assistant to the Library Director, *secretary*

Meeting Agendas and Notes

- May 16, 2011: agenda | notes
- April 15, 2011: agenda | notes
- February 22, 2011: agenda | notes
- January 21, 2011: agenda | notes

- May 11, 2010: agenda | notes
- April 14, 2010: agenda | notes
- February 17, 2010: agenda | notes
- January 20, 2010: agenda | notes
- November 20, 2009: agenda | notes

GEORGIA TECH
Faculty Advisory Board
http://library.gatech.edu/about/advisoryboard/faculty/

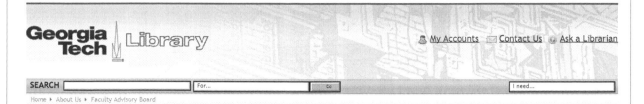

Georgia Tech | Library

    My Accounts   Contact Us   Ask a Librarian

SEARCH [   ] For... [   ] Go   I need... [   ]

Home ▸ About Us ▸ Faculty Advisory Board

RESEARCH TOOLS
- GT Catalog
- Find Articles/Databases
- eJournals
- Course Reserves
- Research Guides
- Library Classes
    - more...

SERVICES
- Borrow
- Renew Books
- Interlibrary Loan
- Library Commons
- Reserve Event Space
- Subject Librarians
    - more...

ABOUT US
- Hours
- Directions & Maps
- Departments
- Donations & Gifts
- Visitors
- Jobs
    - more...

FACULTY ADVISORY BOARD

Created in Fall 2007 by Dr. Gary Schuster, the Library/Faculty Advisory Board (LFAB) is an essential sounding board for the Library, particularly to enhance faculty engagement. Board Members facilitate faculty / Library communications, partner with the Library in areas of common concern including -- scholarly communications, author rights, information policy -- and serve as Library advocates and counselors. Topics discussed at recent meetings were scholarly communications, open access, the Library's institutional repository - SMARTech, the Library commons areas, and Library and LFAB strategic planning. The LFAB is comprised of 20 members with Ellen Zegura (College of Computing) as Chair. The Board meets six times annually.

Left to right: Michael Best, Marlit Hayslett, Bruce Stiftel, Ellen Zegura, Carol Senf, Martha Grover, Harvey Lipkin, Dewey Hodges, Yingjie Liu, Larry Bottomley, Bill Underwood, Andrew Zangwill, and Benjamin Flowers. Not present: Haskell Beckham, Nate Bennett, Amy Bruckman, Richard Catrambone, Haizheng Li, Nick Lurie & Bob Pikowsky

The current Advisory Board members are:

Ellen Zegura, LFAB Chair (College of Computing)
Haskell Beckham (School of Polymer, Textile & Fiber Engineering)
Nate Bennett (College of Management)
Michael Best (College of Computing and School of International Affairs)
Larry Bottomley (School of Chemistry)
Richard Catrambone (School of Psychology)
Benjamin Flowers (College of Architecture)
Martha Grover (School of Chemical and Biomolecular Engineering)
Marlit Hayslett (Georgia Tech Research Institute)
Dewey Hodges (School of Aerospace Engineering)

Haizheng Li (School of Economics)
Harvey Lipkin (School of Mechanical Engineering)
Yingjie Liu (School of Mathematics)
Nick Lurie (College of Management)
Bob Pikowsky (School of Public Policy)
Carol Senf (School of Literature, Communication and Culture)
Bruce Stiftel (College of Architecture)
Bill Underwood (Georgia Tech Research Institute)
Andrew Zangwill (School of Physics)

ACCESSIBILITY • PRIVACY • CONTACT US • STAFF ONLY • SITE SEARCH • GT HOME
GT Library :: 704 Cherry Street :: Atlanta, GA 30332-0900 :: phone: (404) 894-4529 or 1-888-225-7804

ABOUT THE LIBRARIES

University Library Student Library Advisory Board

The University Library recognizes that a strong, high-quality research library requires input and participation from the student body. The Student Library Advisory Board is a fundamental component of the library's efforts to support the research, teaching, and learning mission of the University of North Carolina at Chapel Hill.

Charge

The charge is given in Title VIII, Article III, Section 324 of the Student Code:

> Subject to the approval of the Student Affairs Committee and the Full Student congress the Student Body President shall appoint five undergraduates as members of this board. All appointments last for a term of one year. The functions of the Student Library Advisory Board include: (1) to provide a mechanism for student suggestions to the library administration, (2) to involve students in the formulation of new library programs and facilities, (3) to incorporate student input in administrative decisions, and (4) to solicit student opinion regarding library programs and services. This body will meet on a monthly basis during the academic year.

Responsibilities

The Board is responsible for communicating thoughts, ideas, and concerns to the University Librarian and the Library administration. The primary responsibility of this group is to make suggestions on ways to improve the effectiveness of the Library. Other responsibilities include:

- Determine how the Student Endowed Library Fund will be spent. This fund is described in Title I, Article I, Section 4, Paragraph F and Title I, Article V, Section 6 of the Student Code.
- Provide Library administration with relevant user feedback and advice on library services and resources to support both graduate and undergraduate student study and research needs.
- Provide input on library policies and services and recommend appropriate changes.
- Communicate user needs to the Library, and communicate information about library services and resources to the University community.

Board Membership

The UNC Student Library Advisory Board consists of a group of 10 or more graduate and undergraduate students that broadly represent the academic programs and overall diversity of the UNC student body. Membership is for a period of one year. The Board meets two or three times a semester in the Administrative Conference Room in Davis Library, unless otherwise noted.

Members for 2010-2011

Graduate and Professional Student Federation's Appointments:

Gary Guadagnolo (gdg@email.unc.edu)
AS Doctor of Philosophy, History, College of Arts and Sciences
Anna Krome-Lukens (annakl@email.unc.edu)
AS Doctor of Philosophy, History, College of Arts and Sciences

Student Body President's Appointments:

Nissan Patel (patelnm@email.unc.edu)
AS Bachelor of Arts, Major: Economics
Robert Windsor (rwindsor@email.unc.edu)
AS Bachelor, College of Arts and Sciences
Sarah Kaminer (skaminer@email.unc.edu)

AS Bachelor, Major: Nursing

Speaker of Student Congress' Appointments:

Chelsea Miller (millercs56@gmail.com)
AS Bachelor of Arts, Major: Peace, War, and Defense, Minor: Religious Studies
Joe Levin Manning (jlevinmanning@gmail.com)
AS Bachelor of Arts, Majors: Music, Political Science

Home | Hours | Search This Site | UNC Home | Privacy Policy

Website comments or questions: Library Web Team
Suggestions on Library Services? Give us your feedback.
URL: http://www.lib.unc.edu/about/slab.html
This page was last updated Tuesday, November 16, 2010.

Library **for York U faculty**

Fall 2010

YORK U LIBRARIES HOME

Library Student Advisory Group: Student Engagement At Work

For so many students, the Libraries are their "home away from home". Take a casual walk through the various library spaces at York, and you'll see students camped out in every corner. Libraries are essential to students' academic experience; they are the site of much of a student's reading, writing, researching, thinking, creating and studying. It's important, then, that students be engaged as much as possible in the planning and development of their libraries.

This year marks the second year of the **Library Student Advisory Group** (LSAG). This group was created to provide a forum for dialogue with students about library issues including services, policies, resources and physical and virtual spaces. This year 23 students are serving on the committee, representing a broad cross-section of undergraduate and graduate students from different faculties and disciplines.

Last year the Library Student Advisors were engaged in discussions about issues such as renovations in the Scott Library (the Learning Commons), noise and food policy, and the design of the new catalogue search interface.

This year, LSAG has expanded its role from its original advisory function to encompass project work as well. The students chose two projects, one in each term. The fall project consisted of the Scott Learning Commons Open House which was held on October 20th. LSAG helped plan, promote and host the event. LSAG members were also involved in a Learning Commons Speakers' Corner which interviewed students about their reactions to the newly renovated space.

In the winter term, the primary LSAG project will be to plan and organize an Undergraduate Conference to be held in the Scott Library in March. This small conference will provide an opportunity for students to present their research and ideas to the larger community. (Watch for more information about the conference on the Libraries' web site.)

For more information on the Library Student Advisory Group, contact Mark Robertson, Associate University Librarian, Information Services.

« YULibrary News home

Job Descriptions

```
***********************************************************
```
GEORGIA INSTITUTE OF TECHNOLOGY
LIBRARY & INFORMATION CENTER
POSITION ANNOUNCEMENT

User Engagement Librarian/Assessment Coordinator

The Georgia Tech Library and Information Center invites applications for an energetic, flexible, and innovative professional to join the Public Services Division in this department head level position. The Georgia Institute of Technology is a top tier university and has several nationally recognized programs in science and engineering. The Georgia Tech Library & Information Center (www.library.gatech.edu) is a member of the Association of Research Libraries, and was awarded the 2007 Association of College and Research Libraries Excellence in Academic Libraries Award.

Responsibilities: The User Engagement Librarian/Assessment Coordinator reports directly to the Associate Director for Public and Administrative Services. Working closely with Library personnel across departmental lines, this position will maintain and creatively enhance a user engagement and assessment program that informs decision making, services and learning spaces.

Specific responsibilities include:

*Regularly engage and interact with all Library user communities through formal and informal channels to determine user needs and the Library's effectiveness in meeting those needs.

*Collect qualitative and quantitative data and produce interpretive reports based on them.

*Identify and coordinate assessment efforts.

*Work with Library departments and groups to effectively promote outreach efforts and data-driven decision making.

*Supervise one fulltime staff member dedicated to graphical design, digital media, marketing/communications, and user engagement.

*Participate in service opportunities such as the Information Services Desk and/or subject liaison responsibilities depending on Library need and candidate background/interest.

Qualifications: Required: ALA accredited MLS; knowledge of social, interactive networking, and web tools; strong commitment to outreach and the use of assessment tools. Preferred: Academic library experience; effective communication and presentation skills; ability to work independently and as a team member and to assess and shift priorities in a demanding and rapidly changing environment.
```
***********************************************************
```

University of Guelph Library
Position Description
June 11, 2009

Position Level: Librarian (Any Rank)
Incumbent: TBD
Position Title: User Experience Librarian

Scope and Accountability:
Working collaboratively in a team-based environment and reporting to the Head, Discovery & Access, the User Experience Librarian leads the exploration into user behaviours, expectations, and needs in evolving academic, technological and information environments, and, assesses the impact of user services (technology-based and in-person) on Library users. He or she employs user experience principles* when conducting analyses and assessments and participating in the design and development of new user services to ensure initiatives focus on user success and enhancing the user experience. He or she works collaboratively with the other strategic teams and the Evaluation & Assessment cross-functional team to understand the user experience and improve user success and productivity.

Working within Discovery & Access, the User Experience Librarian works collaboratively with the Design, Help, and Operations work teams to improve the user's library experience by studying users' behaviours and needs, and by exploring new and different technologies, service models, and techniques for the provision of library services in collaboration with the Library's strategic teams. He or she works directly and collaboratively with the Web Development Librarian to ensure that website and user interface design considers a holistic suite of measures to create useful, usable, desirable, findable, accessible, credible, and valuable user experiences*.

The User Experience Librarian participates on the Evaluation and Assessment cross-functional team which provides guidance, consultation, and coordination or oversight for the Library's evaluation and assessment activities.

The Librarian works within the terms and conditions of employment as governed by the 'Collective Agreement between the University of Guelph and the University of Guelph Faculty Association.'All Librarians are expected to engage in: professional practice; scholarship, which includes research, study, professional development and scholarly and creative activities; and, University service and academic or professional service.

Responsibilities:
*note: the time spent on specific work activities will reflect unit and Library goals and be jointly determined by the Librarian and his/her manager

Evaluation, Assessment and Current Awareness 35%

- Evaluation and assessment of the total user experience using a variety of sources, including usability tests, surveys (e.g. LibQual, NSSE), usage statistics, focus groups, and constructive feedback from help desks, other service areas and programs, and directly from users.

- Studies and researches trends in user behaviours, expectations, and needs and develops an iterative process to continually learn about University of Guelph users, respond to changing behaviours and needs, and evolve our services.

- Plans, coordinates and conducts usability testing, working closely with the D&A Design Team and the other strategic teams, to ensure our web-based resources services and user interfaces are usable and enhance the user experience.

- Based on findings of evaluations, assessments and usability testing recommends improvements and service modifications to other D&A work teams and other Library teams that will increase user productivity and success.

- Monitors and evaluates of emerging services and technologies that enhance the user experience and recommends or initiates the exploration into local implementation.

Program Development and Delivery □ 35%

- Participates in user service design and promotes and advocates for the implementation of user experience design principles that not only ensure usability but go beyond that to also determine whether a user service provides useful, desirable, findable, accessible, credible, and valuable user experiences. Works to develop a common goal or vision for user experience in any given project or service development. Considers the impact of services on users and examines the total user experience from need identification through fulfilment.

- Participates in the development and design of content management strategies and actively provides advice to and communicates content development and delivery strategies to content creators to ensure that content development meets the needs of faculty, staff, and students and meets accessibility and Library web site development standards.

- Provides project management for user experience initiatives, defining project components, timelines, participation and staffing requirements.

- Provides reference services, and consultation and/or advice on the integration of library resources and web-based services into the learning environment and in support of research and teaching activities □ providing the Librarian first-hand experience with users and direct observation of barriers and needs.

Communication, Outreach and Collaboration □ 30%

- Works in collaboration with the Senior Communications Officer and the Library□s External Communications cross-functional working group, develops effective communications, public relations, and marketing for D&A services, programs and events.

- Advises the Senior Communications Officer, the service managers, and the External Communications cross-functional team on communications issues raised and uncovered through evaluation, assessment and usability activities.

- Contributes expertise to and participates in Library projects and cross-functional teams such as; Organizational Development; Evaluation & Assessment; External Communications etc.

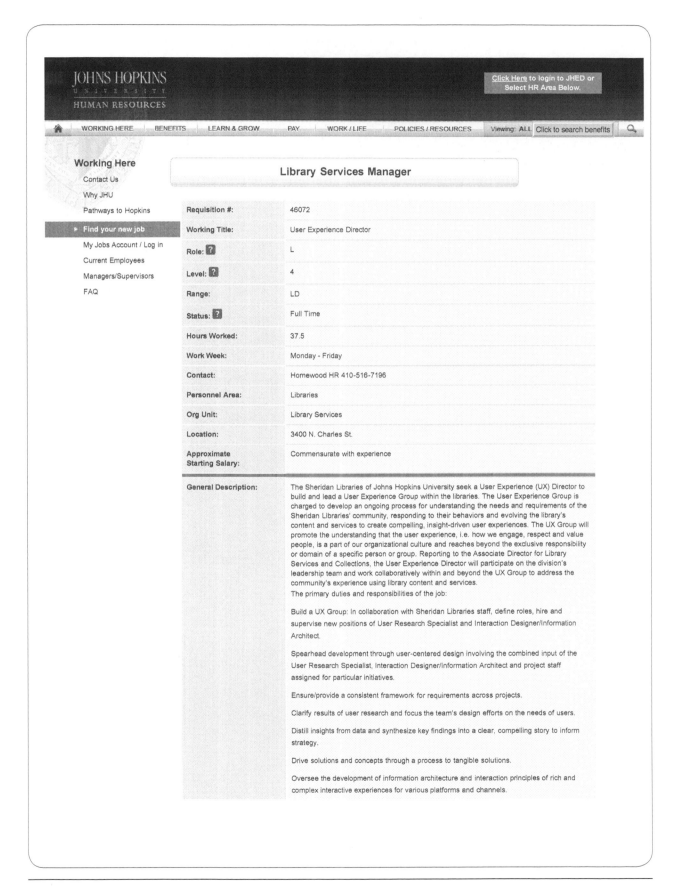

Lead the development of prototypes that demonstrate concepts to current and potential users. Collaborate deeply and effectively with colleagues from a wide range of disciplines.

Organize and prioritize to effectively support multiple projects.

Offer active thought leadership in User Experience issues and trends.

Additional information: The Sheridan Libraries encompass the Milton S. Eisenhower Library and its collections at the John Work Garrett Library, the George Peabody Library, the Albert D. Hutzler Reading Room, and the DC Centers. Its primary constituency is the students and faculty in the schools of Arts & Sciences, Engineering, Carey Business School and the School of Education. A key partner in the academic enterprise, the library is a leader in the innovative application of information technology and has implemented notable diversity and organizational development programs. The Sheridan Libraries are strongly committed to diversity. A strategic goal of the Libraries is to 'work toward achieving diversity when recruiting new and promoting existing staff.' The Libraries prize initiative, creativity, professionalism, and teamwork. For information on the Sheridan Libraries, visit www.library.jhu.edu.

| Qualifications: | Master's degree in a relevant field, such as Interaction Design, Library or Information Science, Anthropology, Economics, Technical Communication, Human-Computer Interaction, Industrial Design and 7+ years in progressively responsible roles focused on user experience. Demonstrated ability to lead the process of designing complex transactional interfaces, taxonomies and metadata frameworks. Demonstrated ability to shepherd ideas from inception to implementation in a highly collaborative environment. High tolerance for ambiguity; ability to prioritize and multitask. Instinct for creative problem solving. Big picture thinking plus relentless attention to detail. Strong drive for achievement, delivering results Experience in managing client expectations. Familiarity with web analytics platforms, content management systems and other core digital technologies. Superb communication, presentation and organizational skills. |

NOTE: The successful candidate(s) for this position will be subject to a pre-employment background check.

Before you apply to this position, please make sure your information is accurate, including attachments. You cannot make changes after you submit your application.

You must log on before you can apply for this job. Log On Now   **Return to Search Jobs**

User Experience (UX) Specialist

The University of Michigan Library is seeking a talented user experience professional to join our newly formed User Experience (UX) Department. We are looking for someone with a passion for user research, the ability to create engaging designs, and an investment in improving the library users' web experience. This position will be a full-time, three-year term appointment with the possibility of renewal.

The User Experience Department is part of the Library Information Technology Division (LIT) at the University of Michigan, University Library. LIT is the library's key organization for the creation, deployment and support of the library's primary web interfaces (Library Website, Mirlyn Library Catalog, Digital Library Collections, and HathiTrust Digital Library).

The UX department will focus on interface design, mobile design and development, usability testing, user research, web use statistics, and accessibility. The UX Specialist works in a collaborative team environment - working closely with the UX Department Manager and UX Mobile Developer as well as LIT and library-wide project stakeholders. The UX Specialist will help drive interface development through an iterative usability and design process. Candidates who have experience in only interface design or usability will also be considered.

*Demonstration of work samples via an electronic portfolio is a plus.

Responsibilities

User Research 40%

- Conducts ongoing discovery of user needs, both prior to and following interface deployment by analyzing user and institutional needs.
- Designs and conducts user research/usability evaluations using a variety of techniques (e.g. formal/informal user testing, online surveys, card sorting, interviews, personas & scenarios, use cases, focus groups, ethnographic research techniques).
- Conducts regular web use statistics and email feedback analysis to identify opportunities for improvement.
- Conducts web accessibility audits.

Interface Design 40%

- Develops wireframes, mock ups, and prototypes to define user interface functionality, navigation, information architecture, interaction, and overall design to help drive user interface development from concept to implementation. Creates HTML prototypes which approximate a functional interface for the purposes of evaluation and communication with the developers.
- Conducts ongoing research into the development of new interface capabilities, enhancements, and user-centered design trends.
- Creates complete interface designs and web graphics.

Project Management & Communication 20%

- Helps to establish project priorities and discuss design goals with LIT managers, project stakeholders, developers, and library staff.
- Performs occasional project management duties including establishment of timelines, coordination of staff, scheduling, and reporting.
- Participates, as needed, on library committees. May provide advice or assistance to other units within the University Library on user research or interface issues.
- Oversees project documentation.

Qualifications

Required

- ALA-accredited Masters Degree in Library or Information Science or an equivalent combination of a relevant advanced degree in Graphic Design, UxD, HCI, or significant professional experience in a related field.
- Knowledge and experience in areas of user research and usability methods, design, and analysis.
- Experience creating concept sketches, flow diagrams, wire frames, and mock-ups.
- Excellent written and oral skills. Ability to work independently and in a team environment. Ability to handle multiple tasks and projects simultaneously.

Desired

- Experience creating complete interface designs and web graphics.
- Experience designing and/or evaluating Library Systems (e.g., digital libraries, OPACs, library websites) or other complex, data-rich websites.
- Experience designing and/or evaluating mobile interfaces.
- Proficiency with Adobe Creative Suite software, diagramming software (e.g., Omnigraffle, Visio), screen recording software (e.g., Camtasia, Morae, UserVue), assistive technology (e.g., JAWS).
- Familiarity with accessibility coding standards, validation tools, and evaluation techniques.
- Experience creating and editing web pages using HTML & CSS or web authoring software (e.g., Dreamweaver).
- Familiarity with XML, XSLT, Drupal, Javascript.
- Experience conducting log/web use statistics analysis.

BENEFITS, RANK, & SALARY

Final rank and salary dependent on experience and qualifications; position is anticipated to be filled at the Assistant Librarian or Associate Librarian level. Professional positions receive 24 days of vacation a year; 15 days of sick leave a year with provisions for extended benefits as well as opportunities for professional development and travel. TIAA-CREF or Fidelity Investments retirement options available.

APPLICATION PROCESS

Send cover letter & resume (as email attachments please) to libhumres@umich.edu directed to the attention of Robert Campe; Library Human Resources; 404 Hatcher Graduate Library North; University of Michigan; Ann Arbor, MI 48109-1205. For further information, call 734 764-2546.

Questions about the job description may be emailed to Suzanne Chapman, User Experience Department Manager at suzchap@umich.edu

SELECTED RESOURCES

Books and Articles

Bell, Steven J. "Design Thinking." *American Libraries* 39 (January/February 2008): 44–49.

Bell, Steven J. "Fish Market 101: Why Not a Reference User Experience?" *Library Journal* 135 (November 15, 2010): 6–7.
http://www.libraryjournal.com/lj/reviewsreference/887364-283/fish_market_101_why_not.html.csp

Bivens-Tatum, Wayne. "Imagination, Sympathy, and the User Experience." *Library Journal* 135 (November 15, 2010): 8.
http://www.libraryjournal.com/lj/reviewsreference/887365-283/imagination_sympathy_and_the_user.html.csp

Brown, Tim. "Design Thinking." *Harvard Business Review* 86 (June 2008): 1–9.
http://hbr.org/2008/06/design-thinking/ar/1

Buley, Leah. "How to Be a User Experience Team of One." *Bulletin of the American Society for Information Science and Technology (Online)*. 34 (August/September 2008): 26.
http://www.asis.org/Bulletin/Aug-08/AugSep08_Buley.html

Diller, Stephen, Nathan Shedroff, and Darrel Rhea. *Making Meaning: How Successful Businesses Deliver Meaningful Customer Experiences*. Berkeley, CA: New Riders, 2008.

Dorney, Erin. "Job of a Lifetime: The User Experience Librarian." *College and Research Libraries News* 70 (June 2009): 346–47.

Forrest, Charles. "Academic Libraries as Learning Spaces: Library Effectiveness and the User Experience." *Georgia Library Quarterly* 46, issue 3 (2009): 7–10.
http://digitalcommons.kennesaw.edu/glq/vol46/iss3/4/

Knemeyer, Dirk. "Defining Experience: Clarity Amidst the Jargon." *UX Matters* (April 12, 2008).
http://www.uxmatters.com/MT/archives/000277.php

Mathews, Brian. *Marketing Today's Academic Library: A Bold New Approach to Communicating with Students*. Chicago: American Library Association, 2009.

Merholz, Peter. *Subject to Change: Creating Great Products and Services for an Uncertain World*. Sebastopol, CA: O'Reilly Media, 2008.

Michelli, Joseph A. *The Starbucks Experience: 5 Principles for Turning Ordinary into Extraordinary*. New York: McGraw-Hill, 2007.

Pethokoukis, James M. "The Deans of Design: From the Computer Mouse to the Newest Swiffer, IDEO is the Firm behind the Scenes." *U.S. News & World Report* (September 24, 2006). http://www.usnews.com/usnews/biztech/articles/060924/2best.htm

Pink, Daniel H. *A Whole New Mind: Why Right-Brainers Will Rule the Future*. New York: Riverhead Books, 2006.

Underhill, Paco. *Why We Buy the Science of Shopping*. New York: Simon & Schuster, 2008.

Schmidt, Aaron. "User Experience on Display [Photographic essay]." *Library Journal* 135 (November 1, 2010): 26–27. http://www.libraryjournal.com/lj/ljinprintcurrentissue/887173-403/user_experience_on_display.html.csp

Walker, Cecily. "A User Experience Primer." *Feliciter* 56, no. 5 (2010): 195–97.

Websites and Blogs

37 Signals
http://37signals.com/

Bell, Stephen. "Designing Better Libraries" blog
http://dbl.lishost.org

See also: "Design/User Experience" section of Steven Bell's website
http://stevenbell.info/design

Brown, Tim. "Innovation through Design Thinking" presentation
http://mitworld.mit.edu/video/357/

Mathews, Brian. "The Ubiquitous Librarian" blog
http://theubiquitouslibrarian.typepad.com/

Nussbaum, Bruce. *Nussbaum on Design* blog
http://www.businessweek.com/innovate/NussbaumOnDesign/

Stephens, Michael. "Tame the Web" blog
http://tametheweb.com/

Twitter Sites

Aaron Schmidt @walkingpaper
    http://twitter.com/walkingpaper

David Lec King @davidleeking
    http://twitter.com/davidleeking

Michael Stephens @mstephens7
    http://twitter.com/mstephens7

Toby Greenwalt @theanalogdivide
    http://twitter.com/theanalogdivide

UXmatters @uxmatters
    http://twitter.com/uxmatters

DATE DUE

DEC 0 7 2012			
DEC 0 4 2015			
GAYLORD			PRINTED IN U.S.A.